Living Nordic

Harmony in Design

BRAUN

Chris van Uffelen

Living Nordic

Harmony in Design

BRAUN

Contents

Preface

For over a decade, Scandinavian single-family homes have enjoyed steady popularity not only in Northern Europe but also throughout Europe and beyond. They appeal to people because of their aesthetics, functionality, and philosophy of life, which captures the spirit of modern living. At their core, these homes embody tranquility, naturalness, and stability – values that many people seek in an increasingly hectic world.

They are part of the cocooning trend, which involves consciously retreating into one's own home in an uncertain, fast-paced world. With their warm, light-filled, nature-loving atmosphere, Scandinavian single-family homes offer precisely this cocoon. They provide a place where you can find peace and recharge. The need for a personal refuge reinforces the fascination with Nordic living concepts, making them permanently attractive, including their clear, timeless design. Typical Scandinavian architecture focuses on simple shapes, clean lines, and honest materials – these houses exude restrained elegance. Generous windows let in plenty of daylight, creating bright, welcoming rooms that convey the so-called hygge feeling of warmth and well-being. The conscious use of light in Nordic countries has developed due to long winters and has become an appreciated design principle worldwide.

Another added benefit is the close connection to nature. Scandinavian houses are often made of sustainable materials, such as wood, and blend harmoniously into the landscape. Natural colors, such as white, gray, and earth tones, create a sense of calm and prevent visual overload. A single bold accent color creates contrast, highlighting the uniformity of the rest of the palette. Many builders appreciate the ecological aspect, since energy efficiency, good insulation, and environmentally friendly building materials align with the desire for sustainable living.

The interior layout also plays a role. Open floor plans, multifunctional rooms, and clever storage solutions reflect the everyday life of a modern family. Everyday life is at the center – practical, comfortable, and familiar. Scandinavian design creates an atmosphere that is not overwhelming: minimalism with soul. Ultimately, however, it is the attitude toward life that this architecture conveys that matters most. Scandinavian houses embody serenity, relaxation, and mindful living, offering an alternative to the fast-paced, noisy world. In an era of home offices and cocooning, the Nordic house seems to be the ideal living space – subtle, cozy, and open.

LIVING PLACES COPEN- HAGEN

Copenhagen, Denmark

Design
Effekt Arkitekter, Velux Group, Artelia

Completion
2023

Sustainable features
Low CO^2 footprint (3.85 kg $CO^2/m^2/year$); Life Cycle Assessment (LCA); circular building systems; healthy indoor climate (daylight + fresh air); affordable, scalable design; use of existing materials and technique; long lifespan through modular systems

GFA
2,230 m^2

Photographer
Adam Mørk

Plans
Effekt

Living Places Copenhagen showcases a new way of thinking, one that is centered around building a better living environment that benefits both people and the planet. Developed by Effekt, Artelia, and the Velux Group, the project features seven prototypes, two full-scale homes and five open pavilions, with a record low CO^2 footprint and first-class indoor climate. Based on five key principles: healthy, affordable, simple, shared over time, and scalable, the concept can be applied to both new and existing buildings. Built with existing materials and solutions, it shows that future technology is not required to build sustainably.

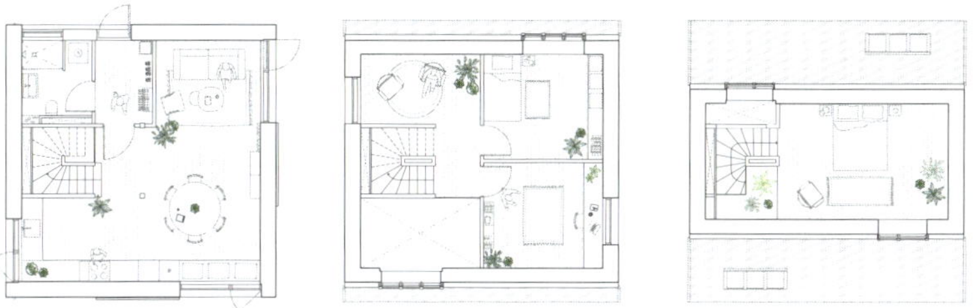

VILLA K

Mikkeli, Finland

Design
Saukkonen + Partners

Completion
2020

Sustainable features
Very maintenance-free; low energy-consuming; long-lasting

GFA
83 m^2

Photographer
Timo Pyykönen

This escape retreat is located on a remote island in lakeside Finland, surrounded by nature. The hideaway cabin is a thought-through entity that adapts to the changing seasons and landscapes. Overlapping roof structures connect the main cottage with a separate sauna building. A beautiful view of the lake is westward, where the sun sets in the evening. One goal was to respect nature and including the building into its surroundings without overpowering the environment. The design was developed as maintenance-free as possible. From a technical perspective, the buildings were designed to be ecological and low-energy-consuming. Materials and color scheme had to blend in with nature.

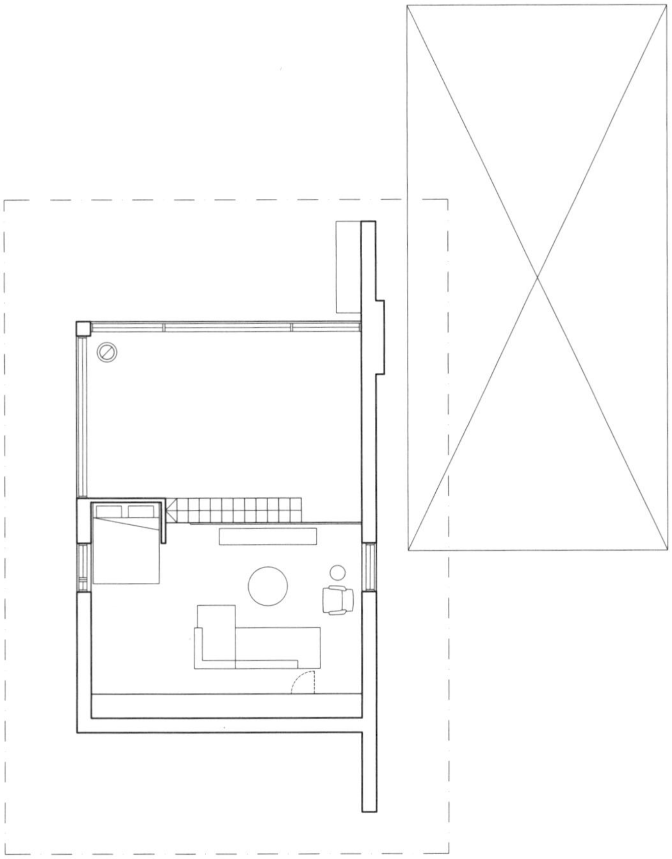

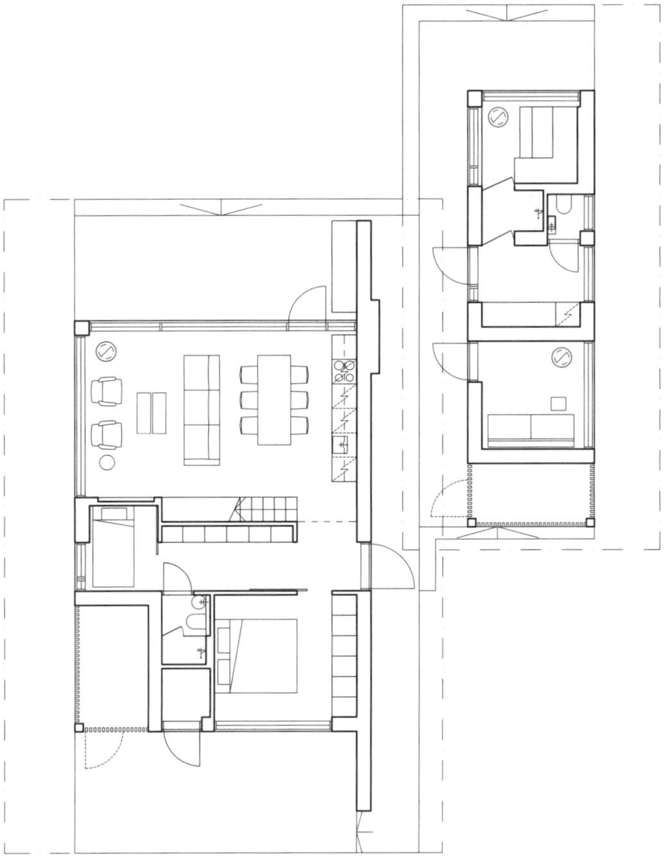

VILLA NÄSET

Gothenburg, Sweden

Design
Reppen Vilson Arkitekter

Completion
2024

Sustainable features
Solar panels; mechanical ventilation with heat recovery; building materials with thermal mass for heat and cold storage; site adaptation to preserve the natural terrain, flora, and fauna

GFA
430 m^2

Photographer
Johan Dehlin

Villa Näset is set in Gothenburg, the second largest city of Sweden. The client, a family of four, saw the opportunity to settle here when one of the last undeveloped plots in the neighborhood was made available. The site is characterized by a dramatic ten-meter elevation change in height and a peculiar plot shape, the result of being a left-over space within the area. The building consists of what appears to be two two-story volumes, joined on the first and second floors respectively and rotated 45 degrees relative to each other. The result is a building volume adapted to the terrain, designed to make most use of the daylight on the plot while at the same time providing a planar surface serving as a terrace with impressive views towards the sea horizon.

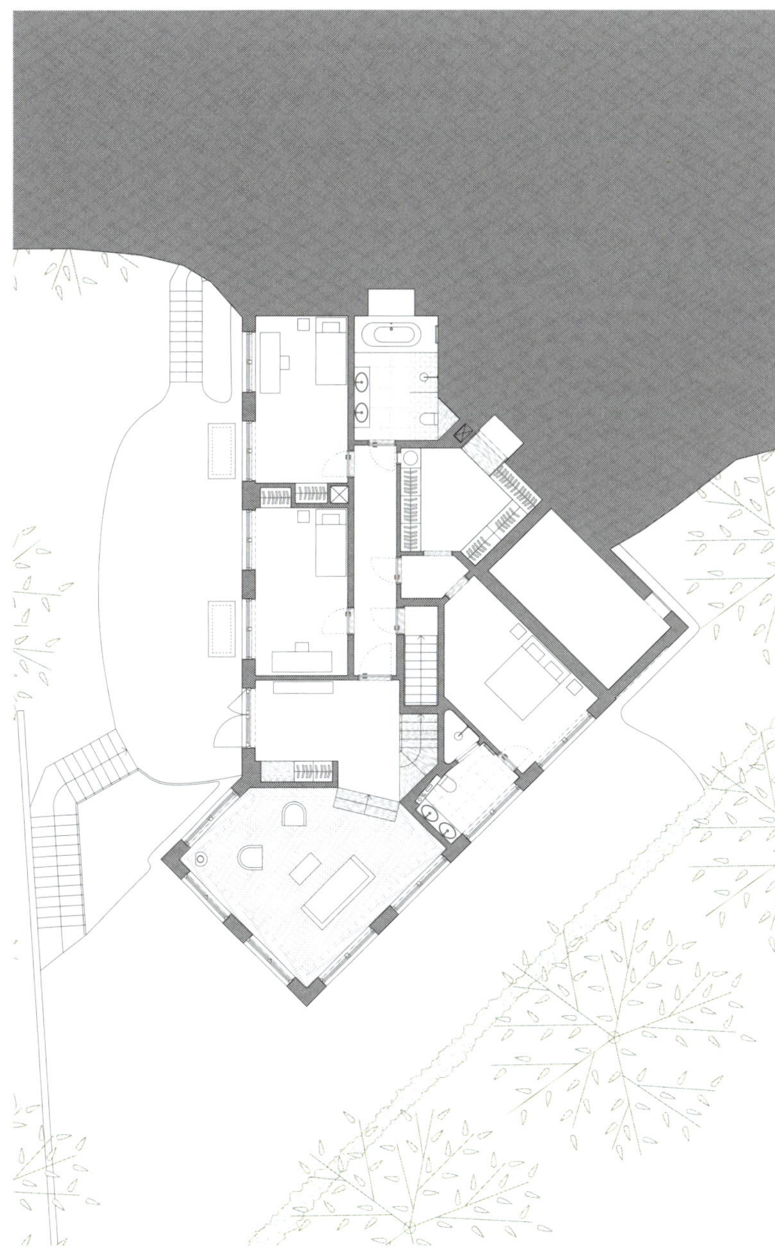

MASSIVE WOOD URBAN HOUSING

Oslo, Norway

Design
Hamran/Johansen Arkitekter

Completion
2024

Sustainable features
Prefabricated CLT; efficient land use; heat pump; water distributed heating; passive heating from windows; well insulated; special attention to sound proofing being in the middle of the city

GFA
630 m^2

Photographer
Nikolaos Farmakis (22), Niklas Hart (23, 24 l.a.,25), Jørn Howlid (24 l.m, l.b., r.)

This five-story house wedged into a corner plot by St. Hanshaugen Park in central Oslo offers three family-sized flats wrapped in a modern all-wooden structure. The urban situation, close proximity to neighbors, and bustling city streets in a listed historic area demanded precise control of the building envelope to meet strict daylight and fire safety regulations. A goal was also getting the most private living space out of the small footprint. The lower apartment is connected to the protected green back yard, while the top two floors boast a double height room connecting the house to city wide panoramic views and the sky above. The special roof with large continuous windows is made possible with a hybrid CLT and glulam construction.

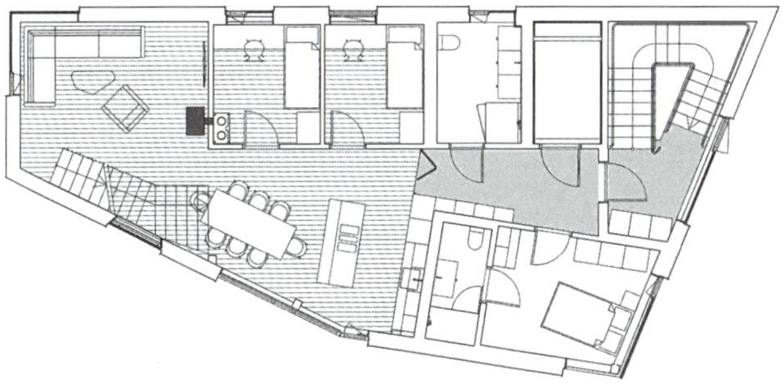

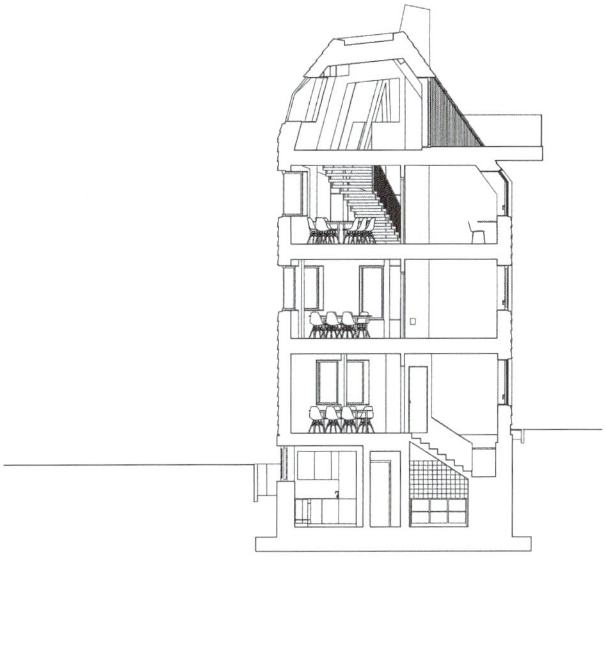

REFUGIUM M

Zealand, Denmark

Design
Ginneruparkitekter

Completion
2021

Sustainable features
Built on stilts to adapt to potential rises in the water level

GFA
55 m^2

Photographer
Niels Nygaard

Ginneruparkitekter has designed a 55-square-meter stone-clad summer house atop a concrete plinth on a small Danish island. The simple gabled form and natural materials minimize its impact on the surrounding meadowland. The concrete plinth protects against flooding and doubles as a terrace, while the stone exterior and aggregate echo the nearby coast. Inside, the house is divided into two zones under a high gabled ceiling, separated by a central glass wall that lets daylight reach every space. Large, glazed corners offer views of meadow and sea, connecting the interior with nature throughout the day. Finishes are simple and natural, with Öland limestone floors and smoked oak carpentry set against white walls, creating a tactile and honest material palette.

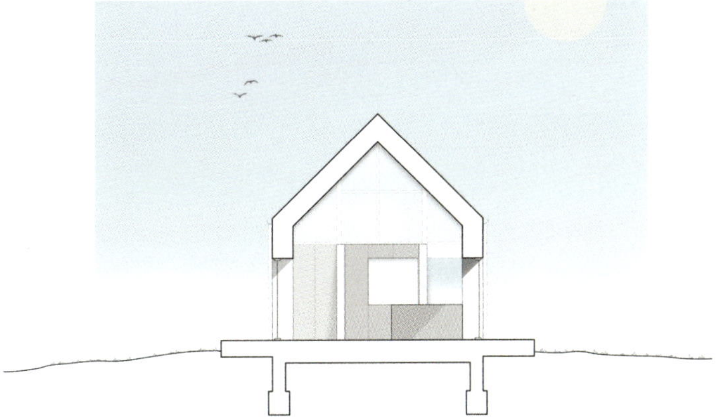

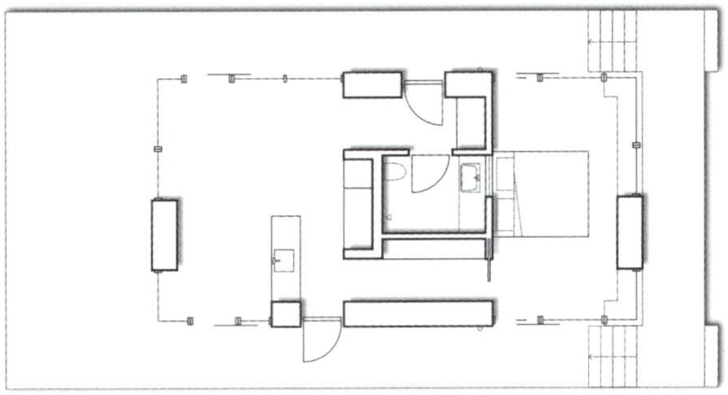

VILLA SJÖVIKEN

Kemiö Island, Finland

Design
Jenni Reuter Architects

Completion
2022

GFA
192 m^2

Photographer
Marc Goodwin

Villa Sjöviken is a one-family house on the Kemiö island in southern Finland. The steep site inspired to design a building on several levels adjusted to the fragile archipelago nature. The heart of the house is the see-through fireplace, surrounded by an open kitchen, dining, and living area. From the building's core there are views in four directions. The bedroom, bathroom, and study are located in more secluded wings, each with its own framed views and soundscapes. The building has a single story, with a floor height difference of over four meters. The wooden building has been crafted to sit in the topography with the façade cladding adjusted to follow the rock surface. The interior has a limited, calm material palette.

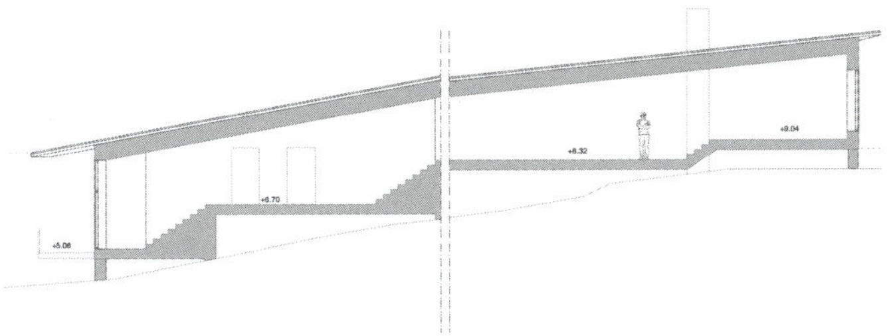

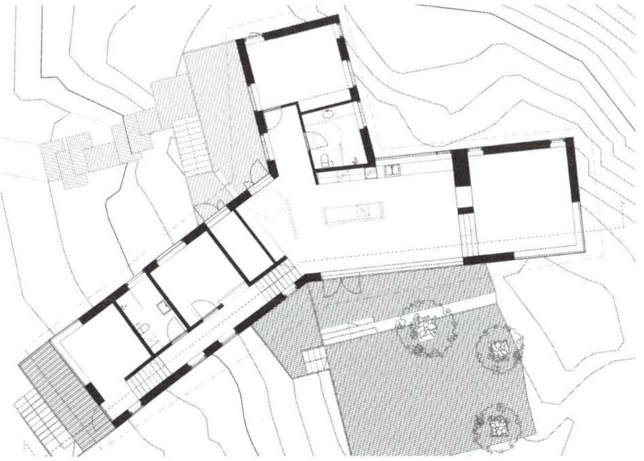

VILLA KIRK

Copenhagen, Denmark

Design
Spol Architects

Landscape design
DesignHaver

Completion
2021

Sustainable features
Minimal use of only few and raw materials

GFA
1,000 m^2

Photographer
Rasmus Hjortshøj

Villa Kirk is a hedonistic space for exhibition, play, leisure, receiving and entertaining guests. The client wanted to combine a Bat Cave with a melted Salvador Watch, raw concrete and Scandinavian simplicity of clean and open spaces full of daylight. Embracing a minimalist approach to materials, primarily employing concrete, steel, glass, and raw wood. These simple and raw elements serve as a backdrop to the exhibition space, creating an environment that values the display of art and design. The project required an advanced engineering solution due to the complex geometry of the lower floor. Together with the concrete engineers the architects developed a formwork solution that ensured a continuous concrete pour and a fluid structure.

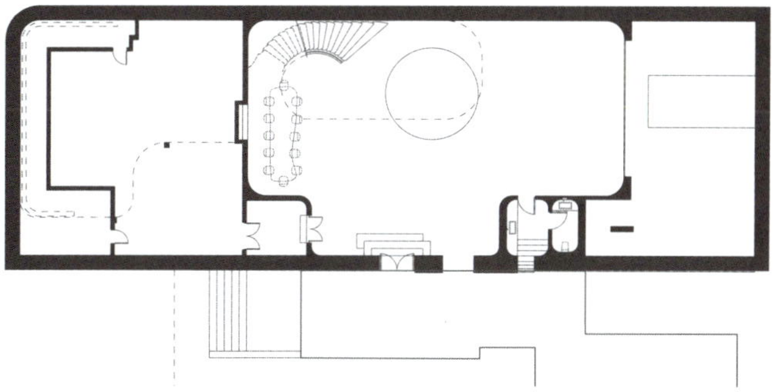

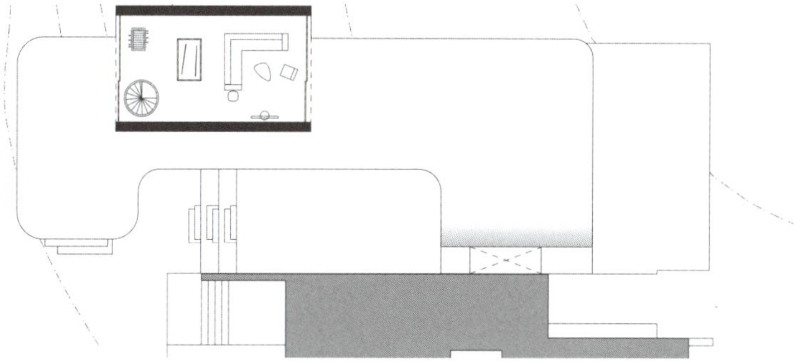

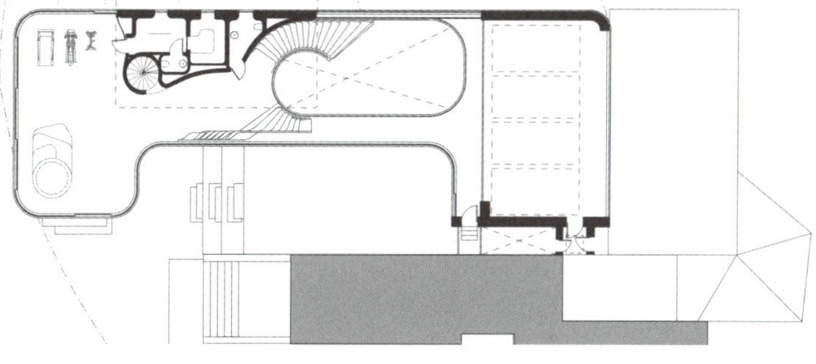

THE BARN AT KUBERGET

Nappstraumen, Lofoten, Norway

Design
Hølmebakk Øymo

Completion
2022

GFA
120 m^2

Sustainable features
Solar panels; wind turbines; backup generator

Photographer
Carl-Viggo Hølmebakk

The building is situated adjacent to a historic smallholding on the Lofoten peninsula in northern Norway. The new construction, a holiday residence, is based on the original footprint of the old barn, retaining its dimensions, yet differing in function and design. While the ground floor consists of the main living space, a recessed mezzanine level above houses the bedroom and bathroom and allows partial double height in the living area below. The south side faces the surrounding landscape, the north side remains closed. In combination with the original barn's history and design, the new program references the history of the farm, local building traditions, and modern spatial qualities. A window above the bed allows a spectacular view on the northern lights.

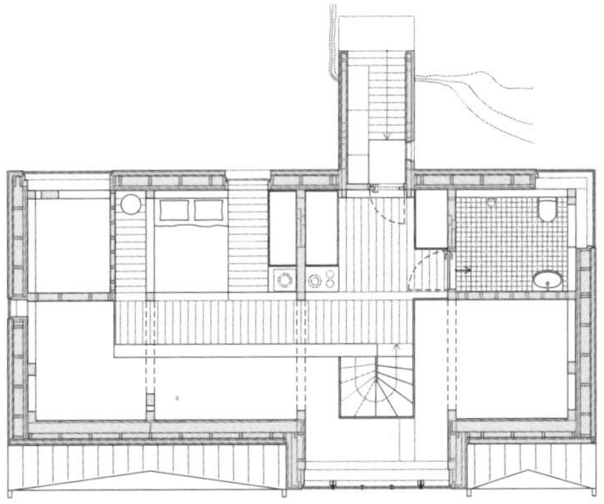

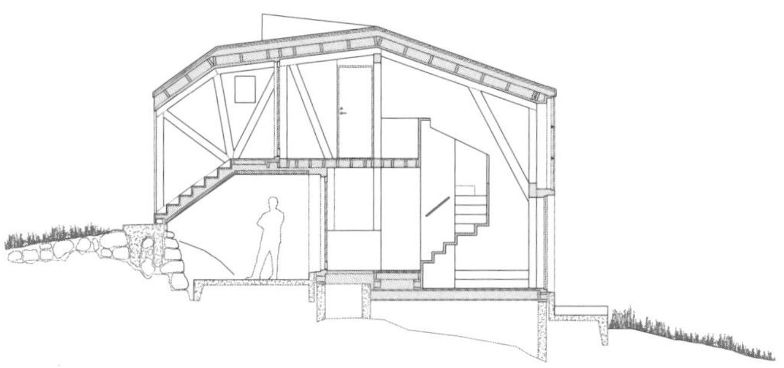

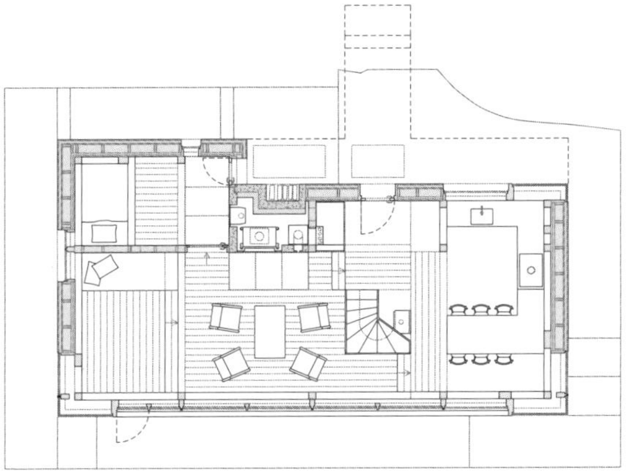

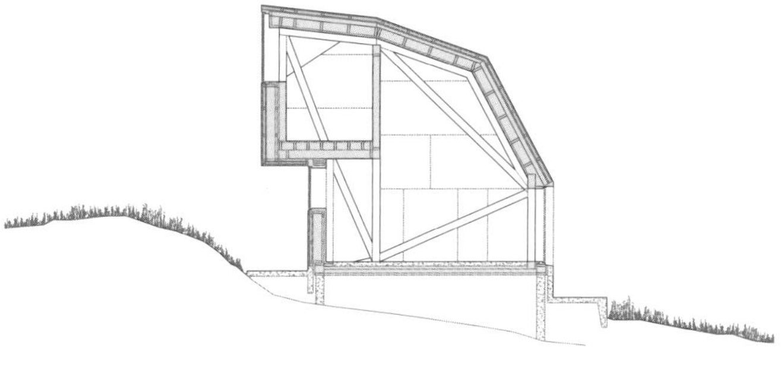

GASTHAUS ERICSSON

Abbekås, Sweden

Design
DinellJohansson

Completion
2023

Sustainable features
Solar Panels

GFA
80 m^2

Photographer
Åke E:son Lindman

Dinell Johansson designed the summer house for their long-standing and valued friend, Björn Ericsson. It began with a simple principle: an enfilade of rooms beneath a roof covered with solar panels. Each room connects to the next, while also opening directly to the garden. All rooms, except the sauna, are equal in size and equipped with wall-to-wall glass sliding doors – even the storage room. Small additions made the principle richer: rounded doors that render the view through the house more poetic, a small recess in the walls to accommodate the door handles when open, and round glass blocks set into the side wall.

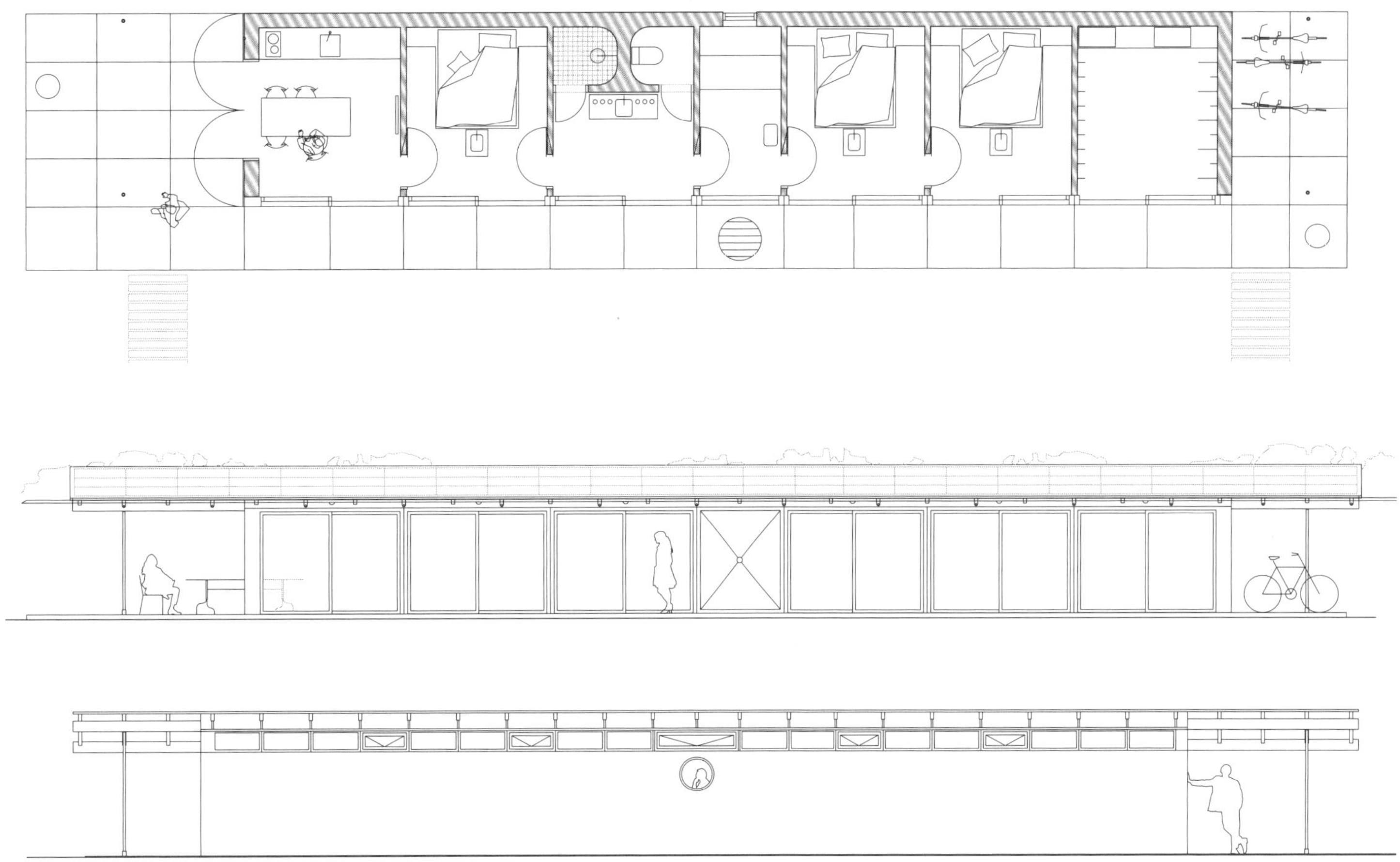

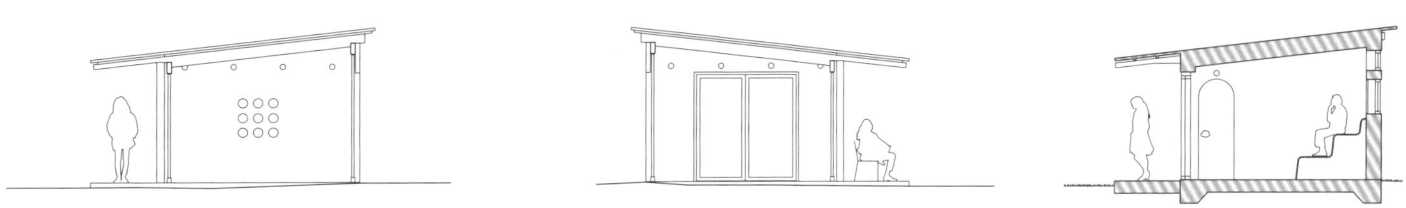

VILLA REKSTEN

Haugesund, Norway

Design
Holon arkitektur

Completion
2023

Sustainable features
Plus house with building-integrated photovoltaics; boreholes and water-based heating

GFA
270 m^2

Photographer
Paal S-N Reksten

Villa Reksten is located in Haugesund, a small town in Norway on the North Sea coast. The building's design is characterized by its concrete and steel structure, which features large spans and cantilevers. This structural design ensures flexibility in both the floor plan and the façade. To make the building maintenance-free, the exterior is clad with aluminum standing seam on the roof and walls. Internally, the prominent materials are board-formed concrete walls and polished concrete floors. The second floor features a solid ash interior ceiling made from locally sourced wood, as well as custom-built black medium density fiberboard kitchen units and furnishings. The outdoor living areas consist of concrete terrace decking, while other areas have a wildflower meadow.

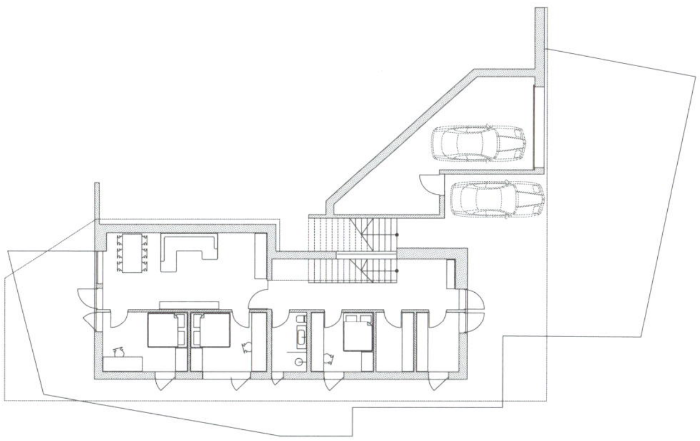

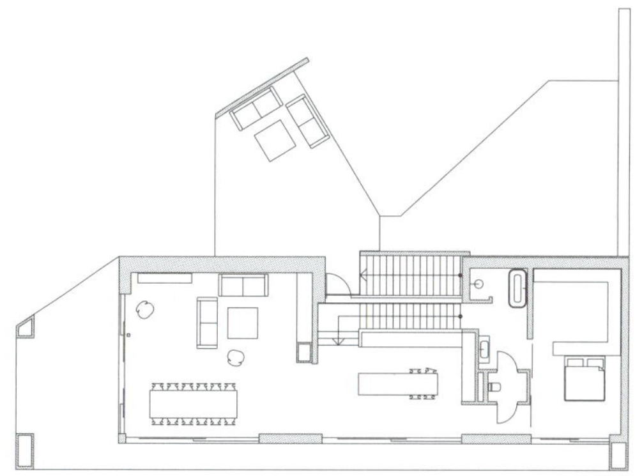

KLÅVA

Bohuslän, Sweden

Design
What! Arkitektur

Completion
2022

Sustainable features
geothermal heating; sedum roof

GFA
188 m^2

Photographer
Viktor Nilsson

Klåva is a local word from Bohuslän, used to describe something that has been split or cleaved. It also refers to the specific topographical feature on the site, a narrow ravine nestled between two ridge lines. The property lies within a nature conservation area, characterized by granite outcrops, sparse vegetation, and a more lush, protected microclimate within the ravine itself, sheltered from the prevailing westerly winds. The architecture is guided by three main intentions: to allow the buildings to humbly defer to the landscape, to enhance the unique qualities of the green and sheltered klåva, and to capture and frame views of the sea. Durable and honest materials such as wood, concrete, and limestone were selected to age naturally over time.

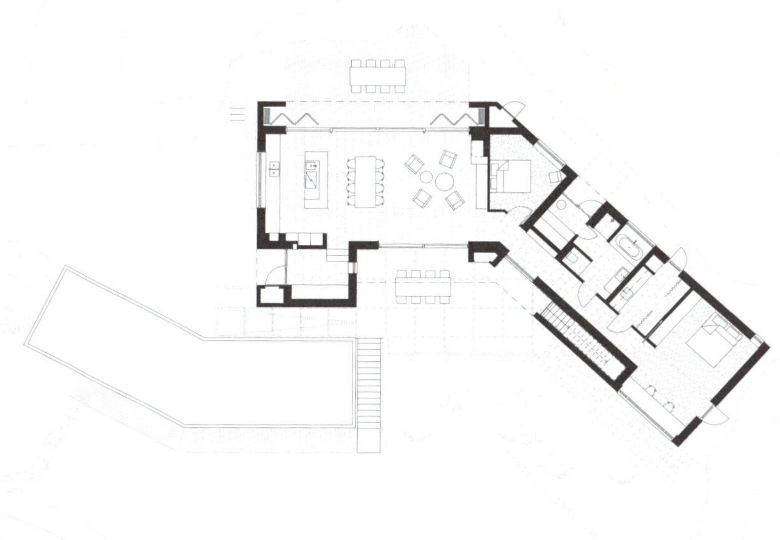

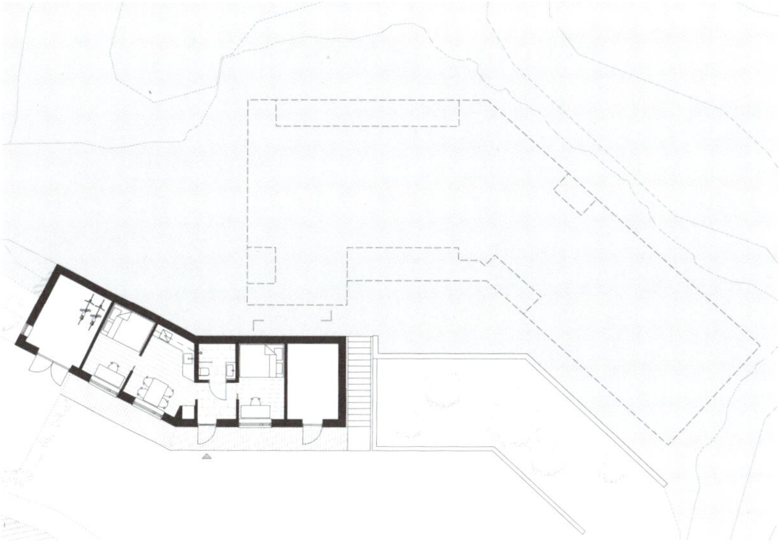

BLÅ HUS

Roskilde, Denmark

Design
Sigurd Larsen Design & Architecture

Completion
2020

GFA
172 m²

Photographer
Tia Borgsmidt

Blå Hus is located on top of a small hill in western part of Roskilde near Copenhagen. By making the house tall and narrow, the view over the fjord and a medieval city center can be enjoyed. The color of the façade makes the house blend in with the dark blue hues of the Scandinavian sky. The main living space is spread over two floors. On the mid floor an open kitchen and dining room grow out into the garden through a terrace facing southwest. The upper level provides a living room with a large corner window overlooking the fjord and cathedral as well as a balcony for enjoying the sunsets. One of the individual children's rooms is horizontal with a panorama window along the drawing desk, the other one is vertical with a loft bed. The extended house appears as one coherent blue monolith.

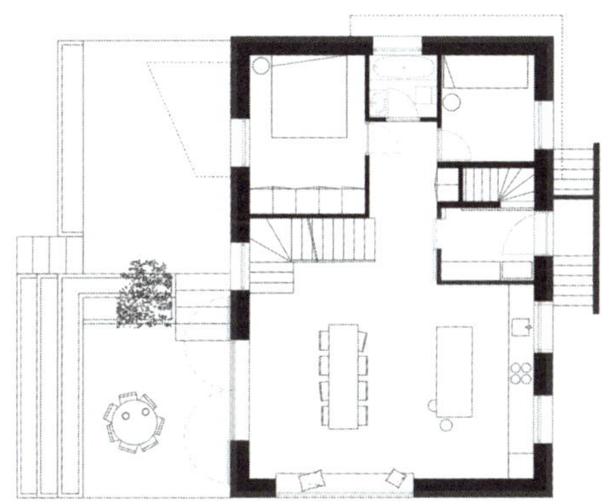

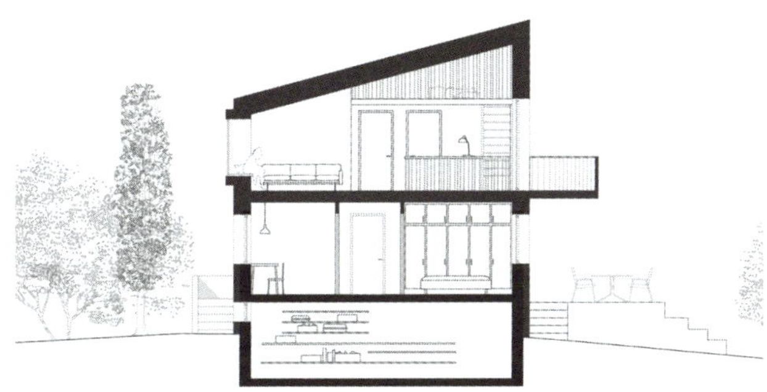

STOKLE-FALDS-VINGEN

Nesoddtangen, Norway

Design
Rintala Eggertsson Architects

Completion
2022

Original building
1970s

GFA
115 m^2

Photographer
Rintala Eggertsson Architects

Stoklefaldsvingen is a home addition and refurbishment project in the small village Nesoddtangen, which is located on the tip of the peninsula between two fjords. The concept was to remodel the initial building and utilize the existing structure as a central hub for circulation into the new sections. The spatial division between the client's workspace and bedrooms proved effective for separating professional duties from family activities. Extending the building in the north-south direction also improved access to daylight and views of the garden, which almost became integrated into the interior spaces through the use of large windows, dissolving the boundaries between inside and outside. To visually integrate the additional rooms, the existing roof was extended.

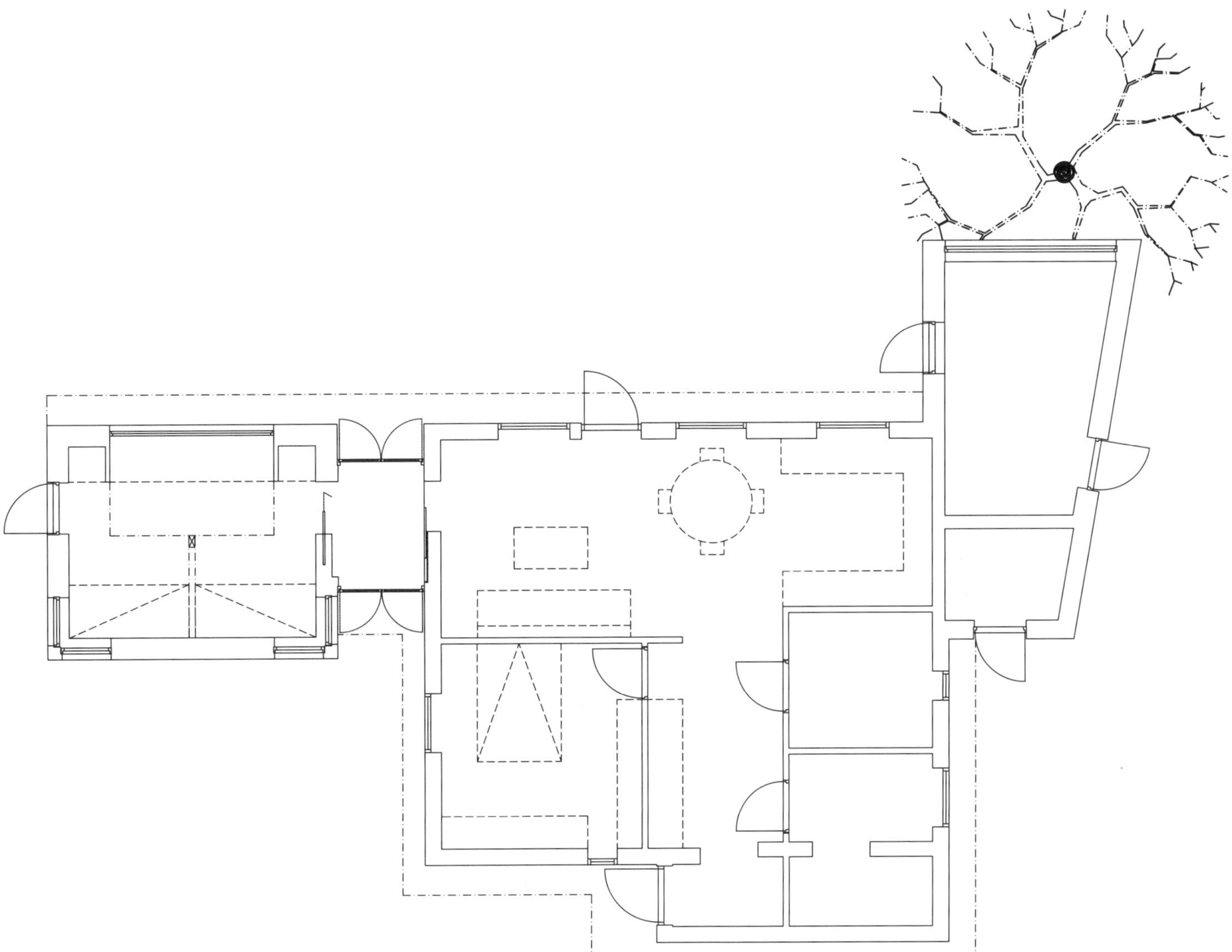

YLJA HOUSE

Grimsnes, Iceland

Design
EDDE design studio (Erna Daniela López Córdova)

Completion
2023

GFA
230 m^2

Photographer
Fernanda Moreno Septién

Located in Grimsnes, in the southwest of Iceland, Ylja House serves as a sanctuary providing familiar comfort. Aiming for a connection with the natural surroundings, the house is arranged to maximize the captivating views of the lake and ever-changing fields through glazed openings. The house blends seamlessly into its surroundings due to a curated neutral palette that ensures adaptability. Externally, larch wood cladding coats the house's façades. Ensuring sustainability, cross laminated timber (CLT) was the material selected. The interior design is shaped by the natural tone of the CLT, adding depth and character. In line with the Icelandic tradition Ylja house is equipped with amenities such as a hot tub.

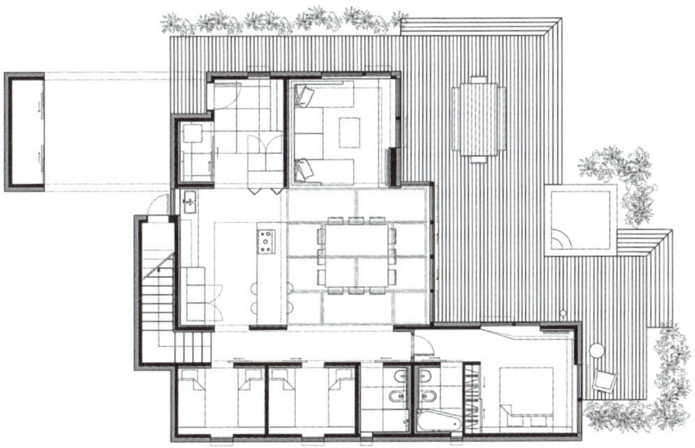

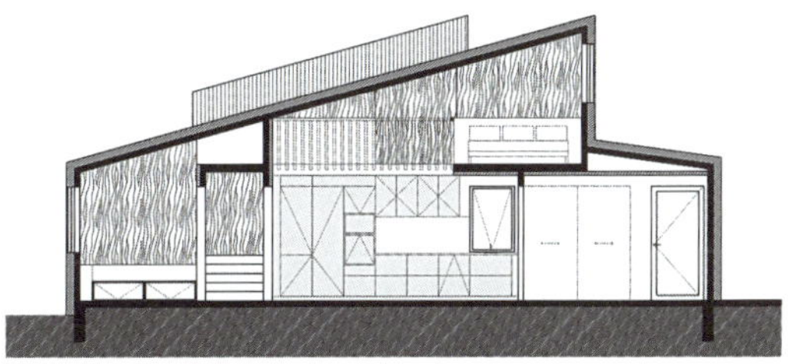

SIMONSSON HOUSE

Boden, Sweden

Design
Claesson Koivisto Rune Architects

Completion
2020

GFA
220 m^2

Further participants
Claesson Koivisto Rune

Photographer
Åke E:son Lindman

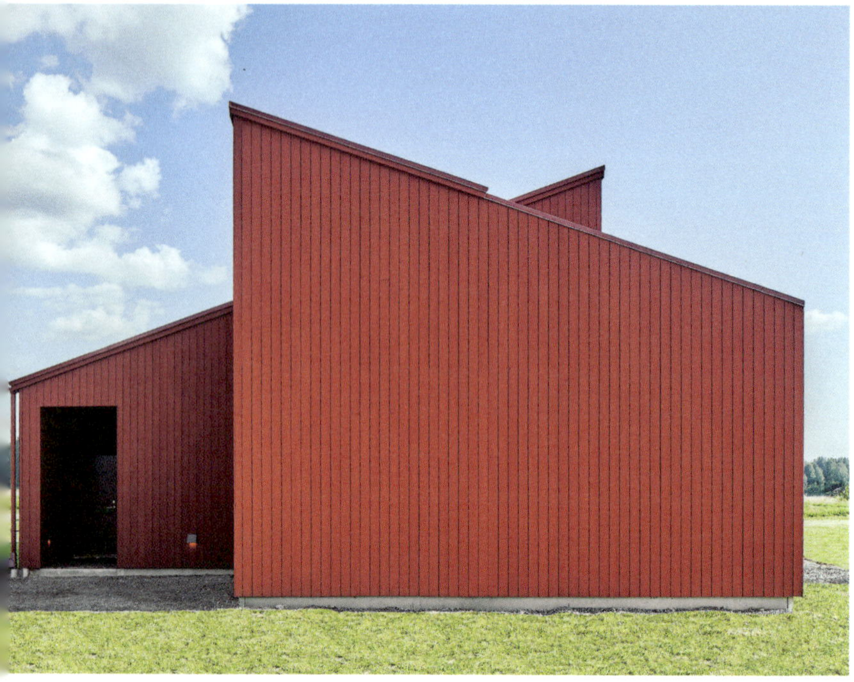

Unusually strict zoning regulations shaped this private house: a maximum height of 4.2 meters and the requirement of a red roof. To achieve a usable second floor, the architects chose a single pitch roof, whose mean height calculation kept the building within the rules. The house consists of two trapezoidal volumes facing opposite directions. The larger holds the living spaces facing the river; the smaller contains a garage, sauna, and roof terrace. Finished entirely in red paint, the house meets the stipulation for a red roof.

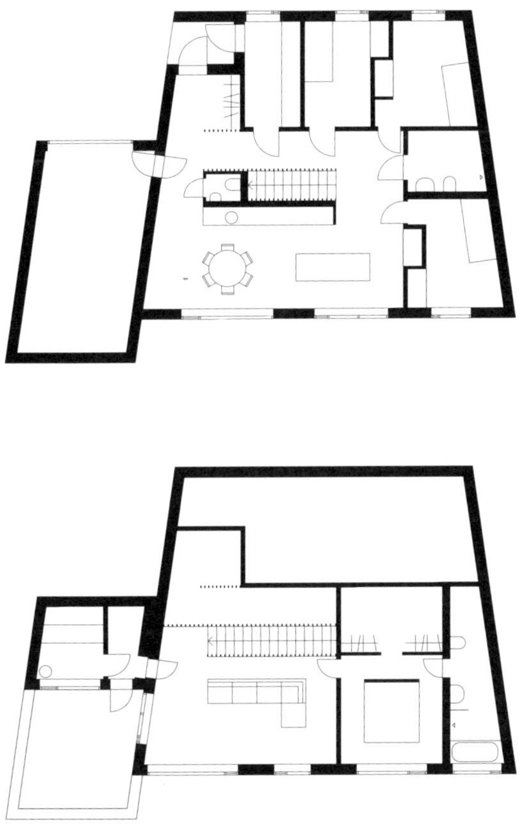

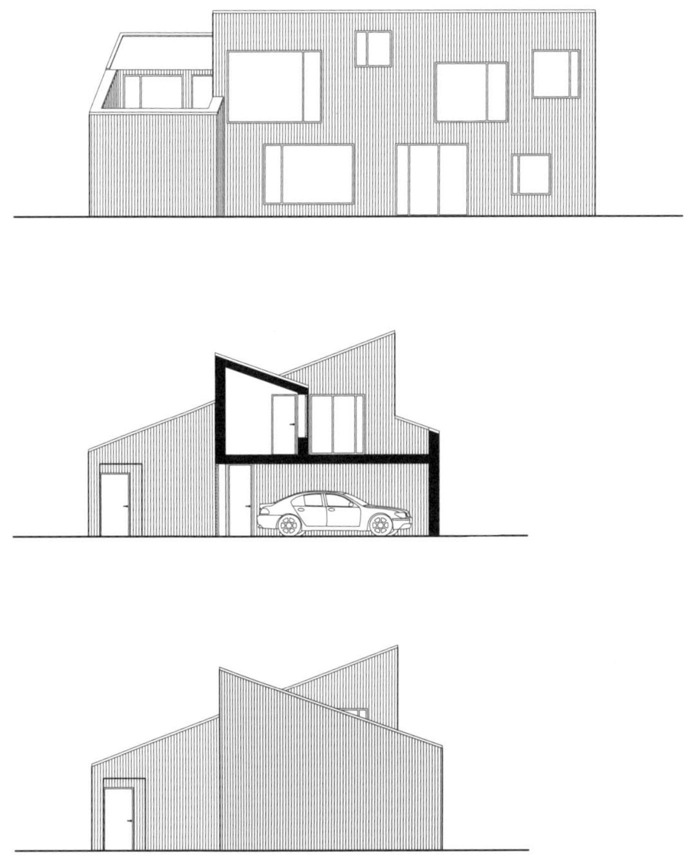

SKIGARD HYTTE

Fåvang, Norway

Design
Mork-Ulnes Architects

Completion
2019

GFA
144 m^2

Further participants
Hafjell Bygg, Strønes Snekkerverksted

Photographer
Bruce Damonte

On top of a mountain in Kvitfjell resort of Fåvang, Norway, is a regular grid of 45 wooden columns. The columns lift a 144-square- meter cabin 1.5 meters above the ground, allowing native grasses that sheep and cows graze on to grow below. The columns are clad with skigard, a long and narrow, quarter cut tree log that is traditionally laid out diagonally by Norwegian farmers as fencing. The roof is overgrown with the same native grasses found on the ground below and on century's old Norwegian buildings. The cabin is accessed through a series of wide wooden steps that lead to a veranda which frames the view of a valley and river below. Internally, the wood cabin is divided along its length into four smaller spaces, each housed under a frustrum ceiling capped with a skylight. The spaces are scaled intimately but open visually and physically to the landscape below and a small grove of trees the cabin is nestled in.

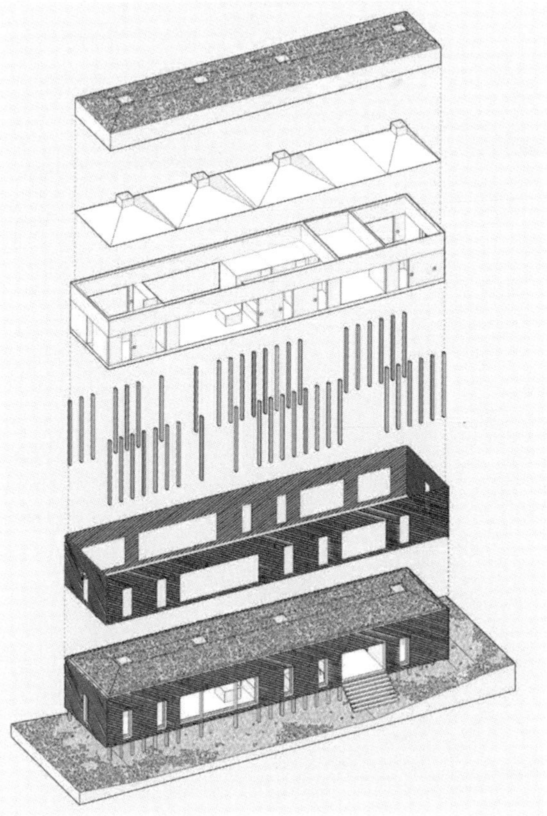

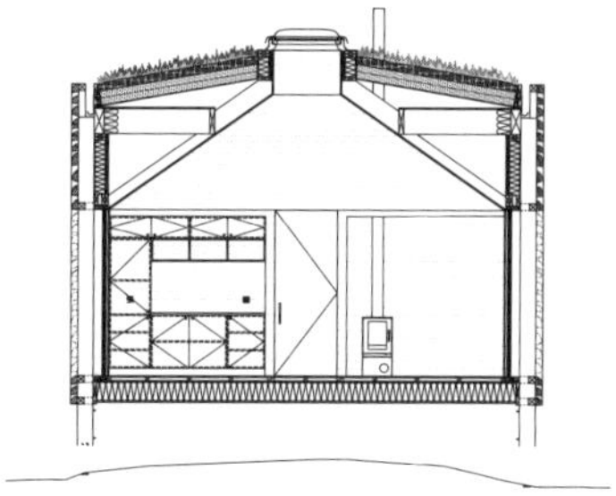

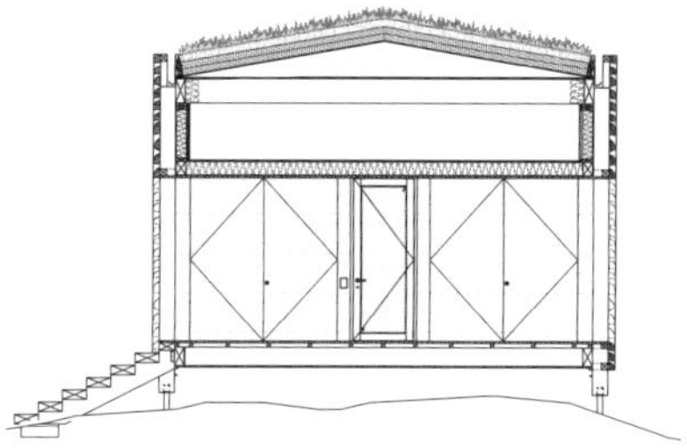

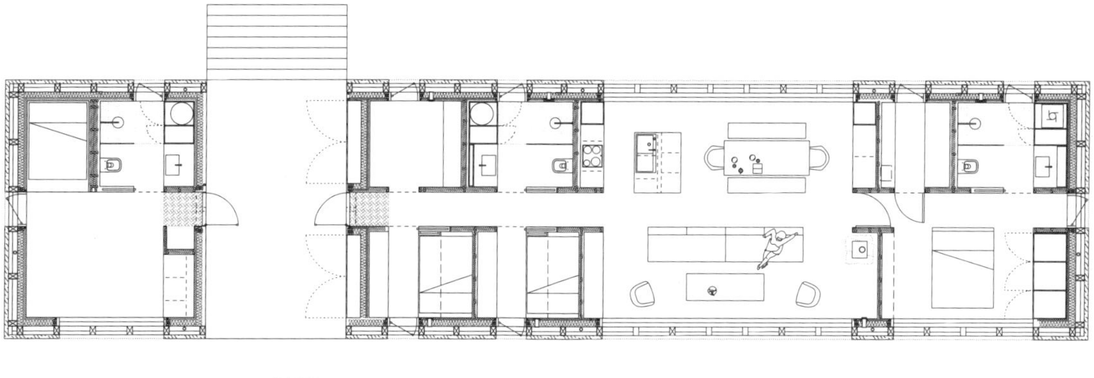

SKOULUND HUS

Hals, Denmark

Design
N+P Arkitektur

Completion
2024

Sustainable features
Charred wood façade; green roof

GFA
151 m^2

Photographer
N+P Arkitektur

Along the east coast of North Jutland, this discreet holiday home is gently integrated into the landscape. From the site, there are wide views across open meadows and out toward the sea. The house is designed in an L-shape, embracing a sheltered, southwest-facing courtyard. Its façade is covered in charred wood – an old technique used to preserve wood. Together with cast concrete chimneys and a green roof, the house appears both rustic and full of character. The dark exterior contrasts with the light maple interior, creating a calm and inviting atmosphere. A modern retreat that blends tradition with quiet simplicity.

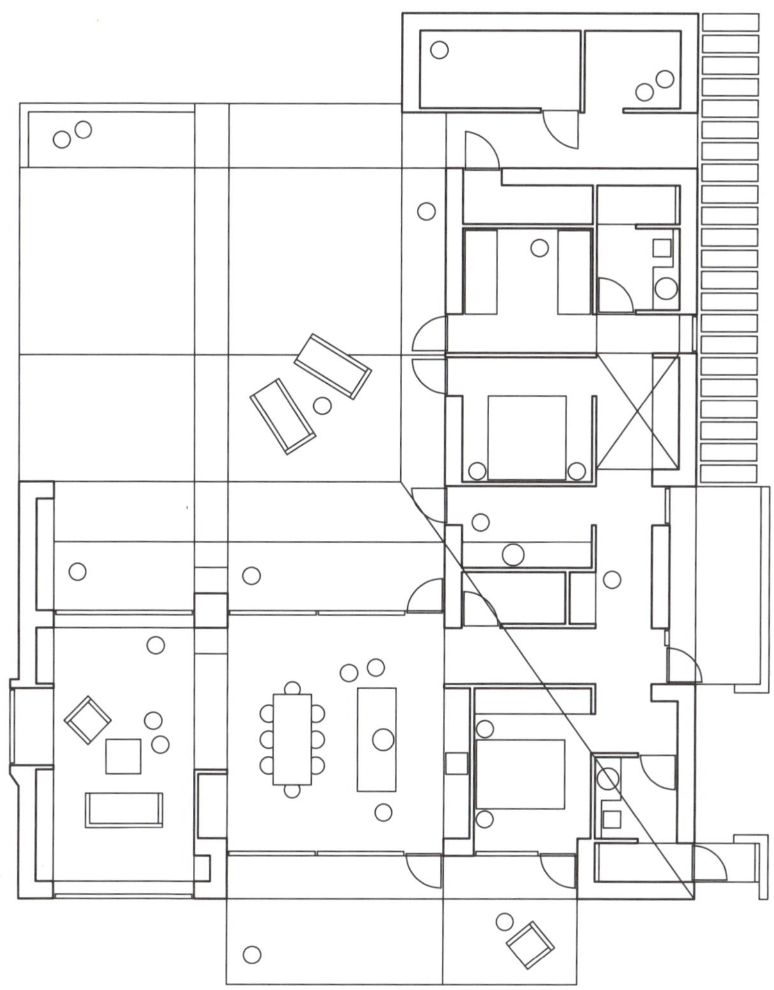

WEEKEND HOUSE HJELTNES

Mandal, Norway

Design
Knut Hjeltnes Architects

Completion
2021

Sustainable features
No plastics; wool fiber insulation; minimal materials; minimal groundwork; incinerating toilet; water well on site; only one tree cut; only screwed for dismantling

GFA
60 m^2

Photographer
Knut Hjeltnes

The Weekend House Hjeltnes is located in the center of a roadless small island in Norway's southernmost archipelago and can be reached by a combined row- and sailboat. The views are of greenery, tree trunks, and walls of bare rock. The program is divided in three separate buildings, a main cabin, an annex, and a shed. All three buildings share the same general concept, but nuances occur according to their different uses. The main cabin has a combined kitchen and living room with two lofts providing sleeping on tatami mats/futon mattresses. The annex is primarily a guest house, divided by an outdoor covered living room. The projects aim was high quality, low cost, and minimal ecological impact. This was achieved mainly by reducing the built volume.

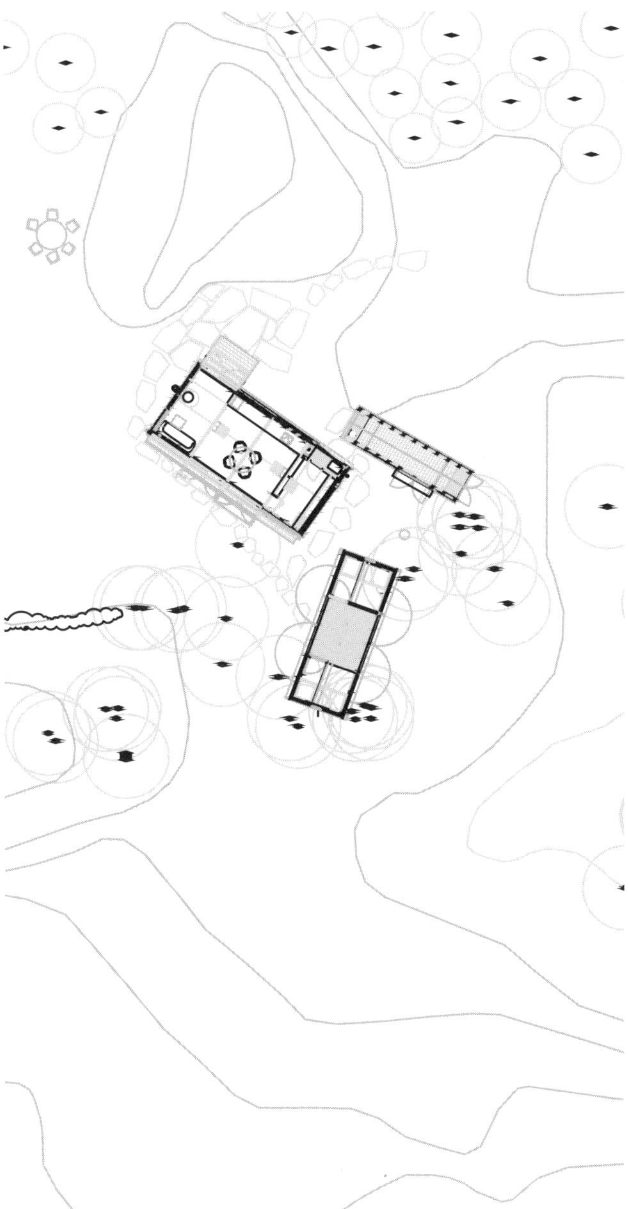

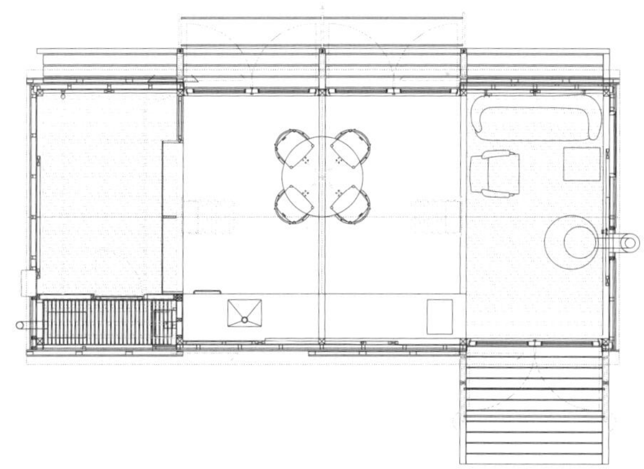

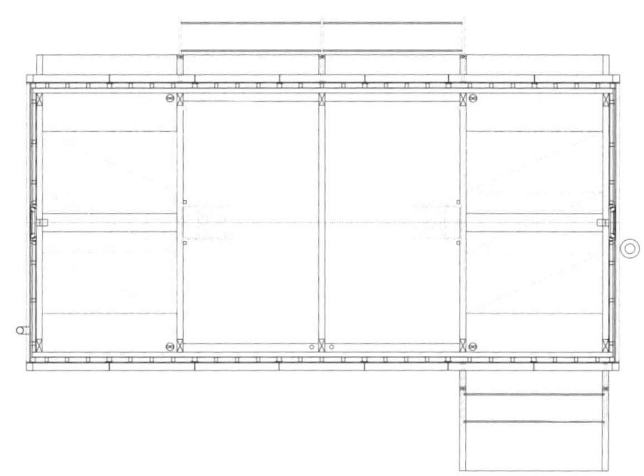

HOUSE ON THE MEADOW

Oulu, Finland

Design
PAVE Architects

Completion
2022

GFA
280 m^2

Photographer
Heikki Salmi/Kaari Photography

Nestled on the grounds of a former horse farm, the House on the Meadow was envisioned from the start as a seamless extension of its surrounding landscape. The building's long, narrow frames echo the open expanse of the meadow, drawing the outdoors in, and allowing the landscape to include into the home. The detached house consists of three distinct volumes forming a small courtyard that opens to the landscape. The main house spans two floors, while the sauna and garage are in separate buildings. Interiors are oriented to maximize northeast-southwest views. Elegance is achieved through slender building forms and a contrast of materials: plastered façades along the sides and corten steel at the ends. The summer ambiance evokes a distinctly Tuscan feel.

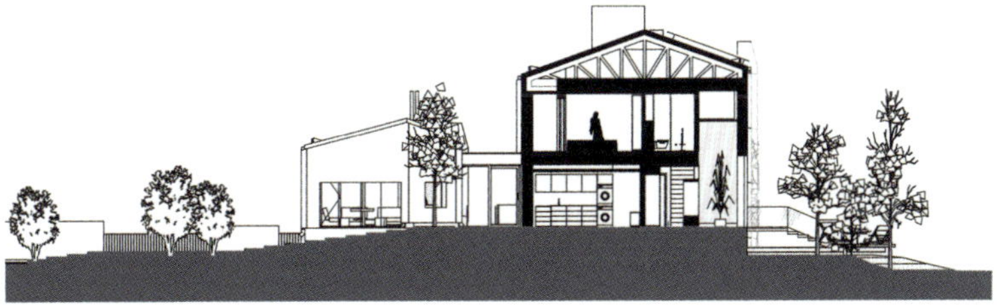

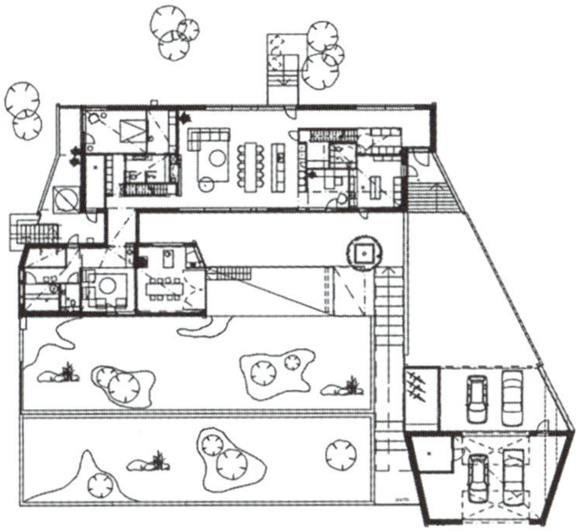

HOUSE ON A HILL

Värmdö, Stockholm Archipelago, Sweden

Design
Tham & Videgård Arkitekter

Completion
2022

Sustainable features
Geothermal energy; solar panels

GFA
479 m^2

Further participants
Ramböll, Johan Paju

Photographer
Åke E:son Lindman

The house is located on a large plot on Värmdö, only twenty minutes from central Stockholm. The site stretches from a boathouse at the waterline up a steep forest slope to a plateau where the main house stands. Approached from below, the elevated position unfolds with wide views over the archipelago. Cast entirely in concrete, the vertical structure anchors to the bedrock like a lighthouse. Organized over three levels, it places entrance and services below, social spaces on the middle terrace, and private rooms at the top. The rotated façade creates a labyrinthine effect, while folded terraces provide sheltered outdoor spaces that follow the movement of the sun. From a distance, the pleated volume appears at once solid and transparent.

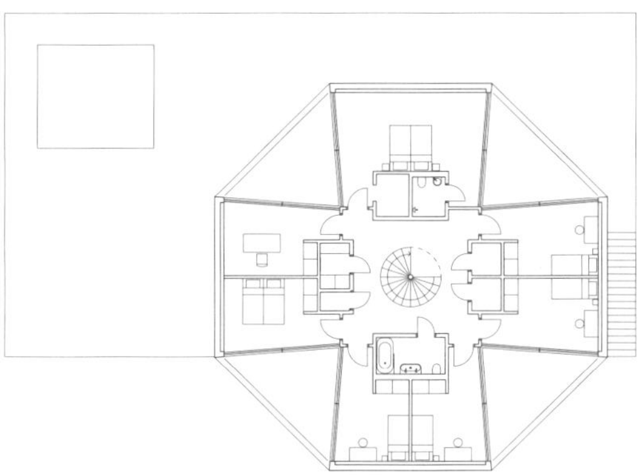

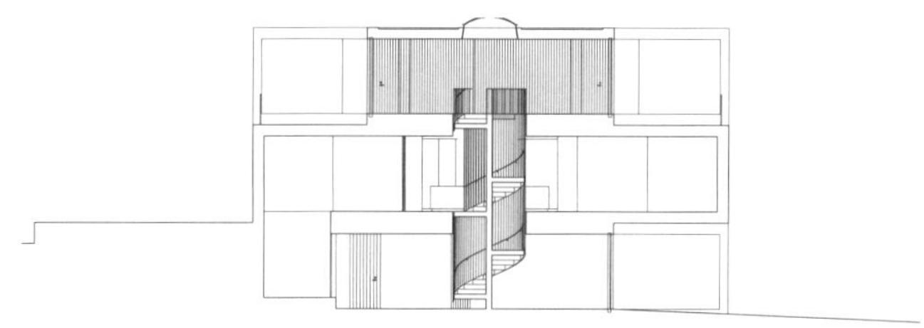

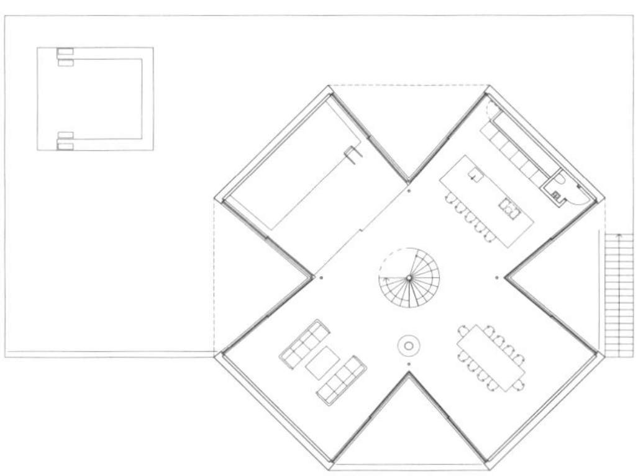

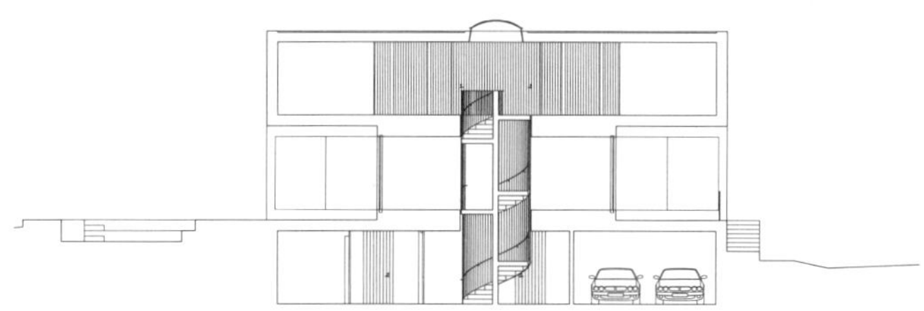

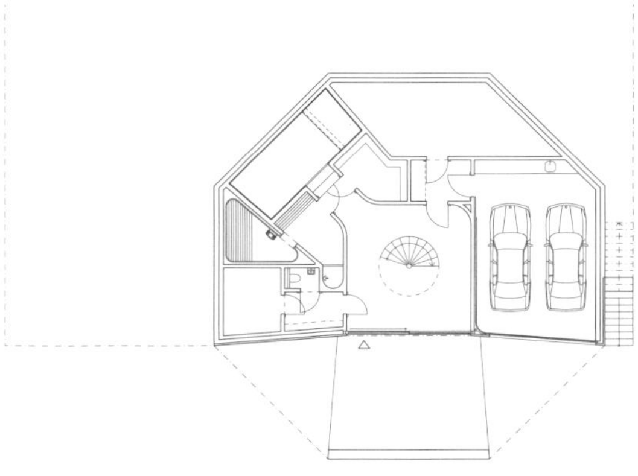

SUMMER-HOUSE

Rørvig, Denmark

Design
Elkiær + Ebbeskov arkitekter

Completion
2018

Sustainable features
Made fully of wood with high insulated windows

GFA
138 m^2

Photographer
Stamers Kontor

Nestled in a private and scenic plot in Rørvig, this summer house features distinct volumes defined by two high, sweeping roofs that weave between tall trees. These roofs create spaces with views and intimate terraces, offering sunlight throughout the day – both in the morning and evening. The house's concept, called Dancing Cubes, generates a sequence of varied rooms and creates a natural flow from the entrance to the kitchen. The outdoor dining area extends the kitchen and garden, forming an inviting space for social gatherings while maintaining a strong connection with the indoors. All materials are low maintenance: the façade is clad in cedar wood, while the interiors feature Douglas fir treated with white oil for protection and a radiant finish.

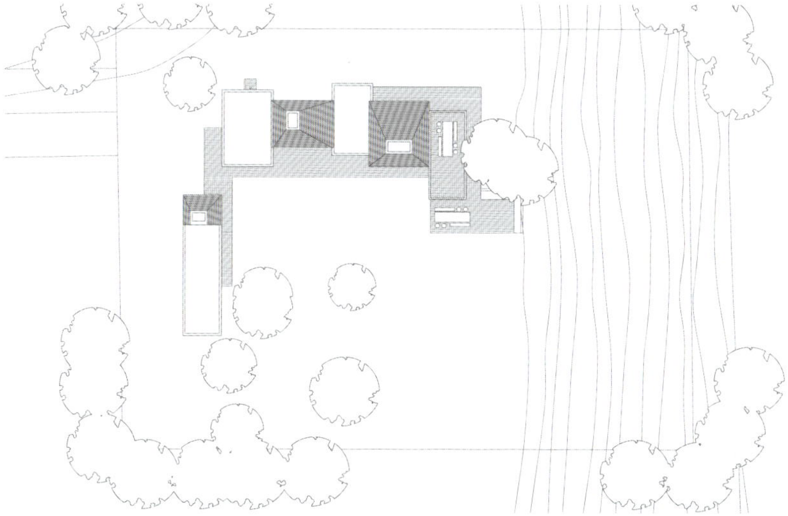

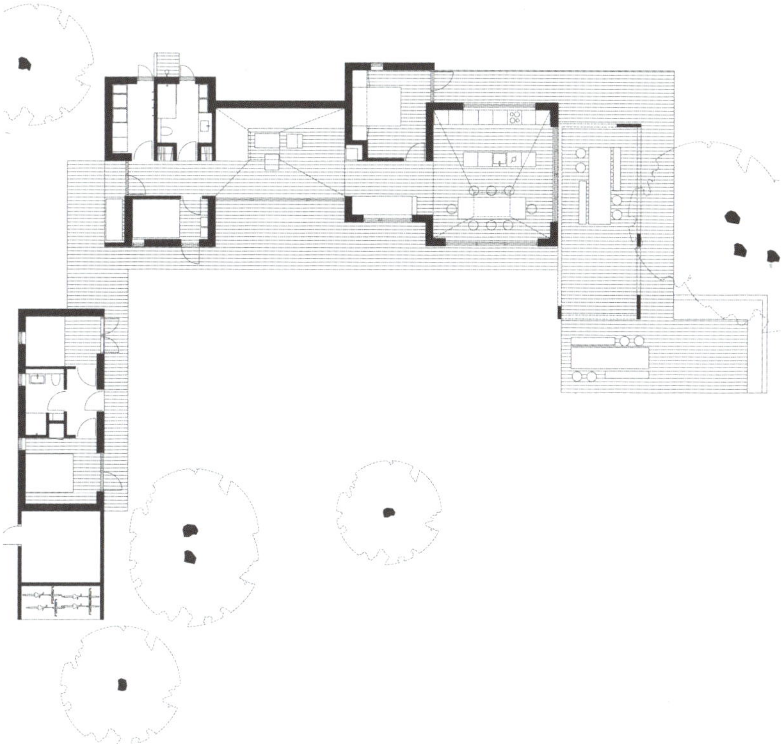

TWIN HOUSES

Nærsnes, Norway

Design
Reiulf Ramstad Arkitekter

Completion
2022

Sustainable features
Efficient space planning; minimized site disturbance; high degree of consistency in materials and design details

GFA
390 m^2

Photographer
Kristian Aalerud

The project is located at Nærsnes and comprises two distinct residences that offer independent living spaces while maintaining a sense of privacy. Nestled within the picturesque rolling terrain, it redefines coastal living by blending with the natural surroundings and paying homage to the area's maritime history. The inspiration are traditional boathouses. Within these angular black structures there is an open-concept kitchen, living, and dining areas on the ground floor. A central wooden staircase gracefully ascends to the upper floor, where sleeping quarters and more private spaces of bedrooms, bathrooms and lounge await. The placement of these residences adheres to a combination of overarching regulations and careful consideration of the property's unique terrain.

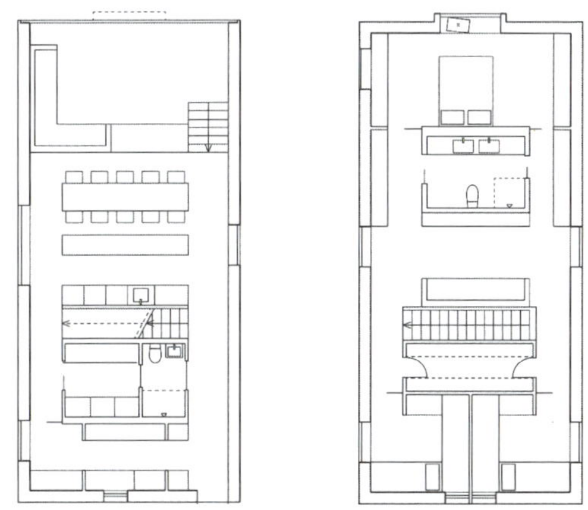

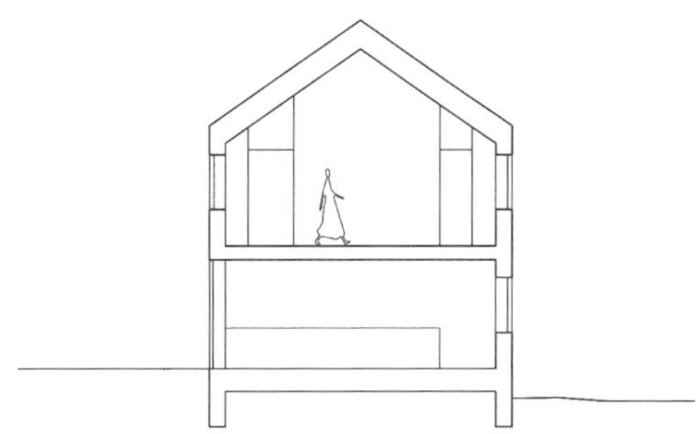

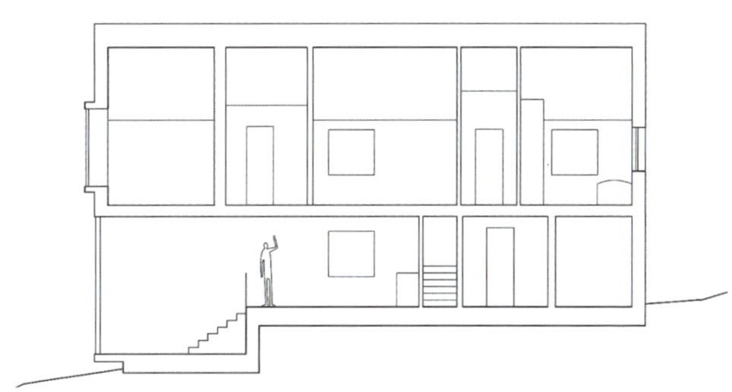

RAVINE HOUSE

Skurusundet, Sweden

Design
Kolman Boye Architects

Completion
2024

Sustainable features
Renewable materials; particularly pinewood

GFA
150 m^2

Photographer
Johan Dehlin

Ravine house is located northwest of the Skurusundet strait, surrounded by a deep ravine bordered by cliffs. It offers views of the Stockholm port inlet. The building is a strict three-story structure with a compact plan that leaves a minimal footprint. By partially embedding the building into the cliff-side, the necessary height for an additional story was achieved. A central timber stair ties the three floors of the building together. The middle floor serves as the main entrance floor, holding wardrobes and bedrooms. The fully glazed, open-plan top floor offers striking views and is designed for a combined kitchen and living room. Each floor has direct access to different levels of the terraced rock garden. Renewable materials were used, such as knotty pinewood, made knotless.

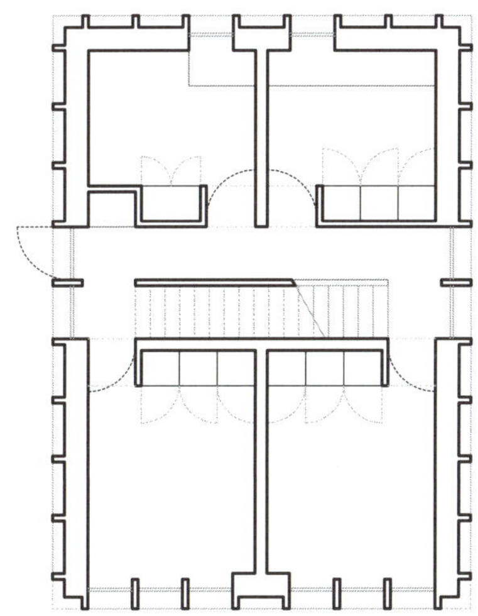

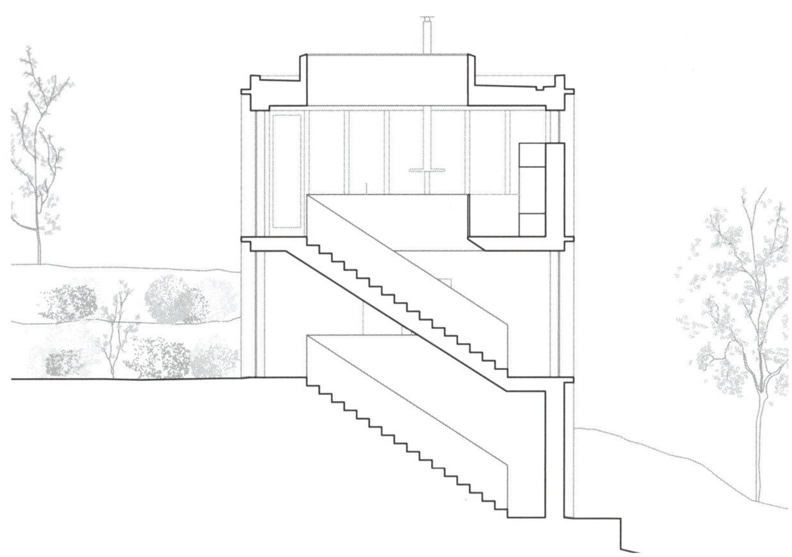

THE SEASIDE VILLA

Aarhus, Denmark

Design
CEBRA

Completion
2020

GFA
500 m^2

Photographer
Mikkel Frost

The Seaside Villa in Risskov in Aarhus with an undulating roof provides stunning views of Aarhus Bay. The design turns the villa into an inhabitable sculpture that takes on a different shape depending on your point of view and the capricious coastal weather. The lower-level houses ancillary spaces, while the upper level contains primary living spaces as well as curved and straight roof shapes. The eaves reduce the thermal stress on the central space's glass façades and create generous, roofed outdoor areas protected from the elements. The exterior features classic Danish Kolumba bricks, while the interior's warm wooden details evoke a welcoming atmosphere. Norwegian slate covers all floors, creating cohesion between inside and outside spaces.

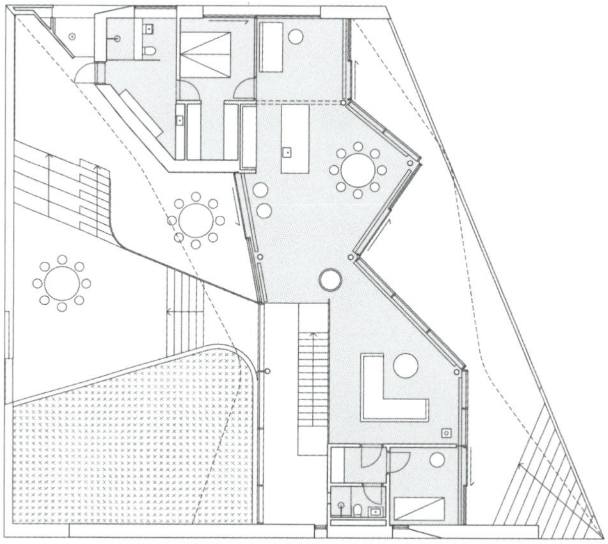

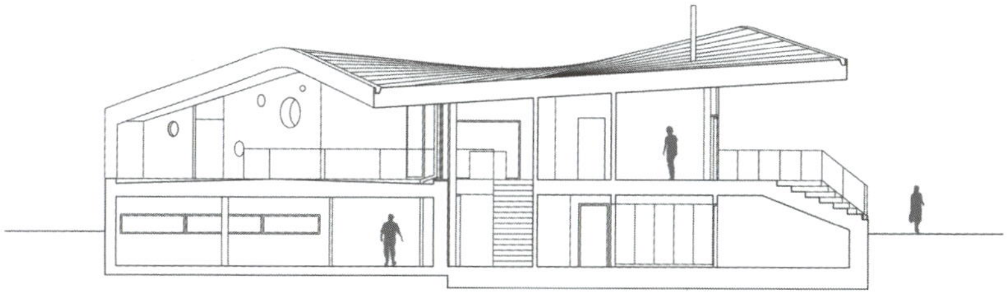

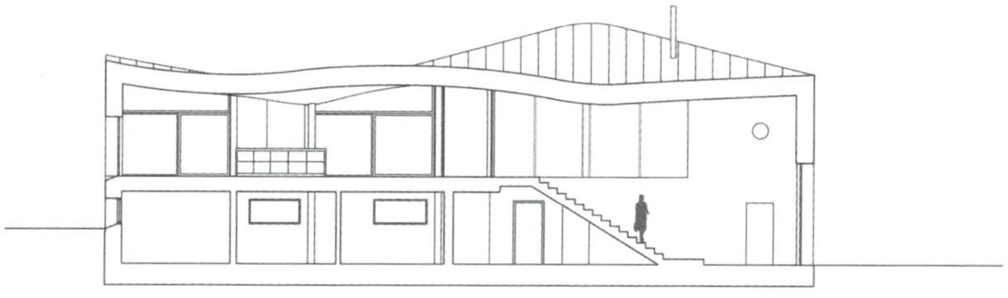

MAJAMAJA OFF-GRID VILLAGE

Helsinki, Finland

Design
Littow architectes

Furniture design
Joska Heikkilä, Pekka Littow

Interieur decoration
Päivi Meuronen

Completion
2024

GFA
92 m^2

Photographer
Joonas Linkola (116, 118 l.m., r.,119 l.), Chikako Harada (117, 118 l.a.), Pekka Littow (118 l.b.)

Majamaja Village is a collection of off-grid cabins in the Helsinki archipelago, transported without road access and built around a patented sanitary-kitchen module with energy storage and wastewater treatment. Conceived by Finnish architect Pekka Littow, it responds to the trend of sustainable living inspired by traditional housing and harmony with nature. The cabins combine modern design with solid wood construction, integrated storage, fold-away furniture, and minimalist finishes. Prefabricated elements allow easy assembly, disassembly, and relocation, even in remote areas.

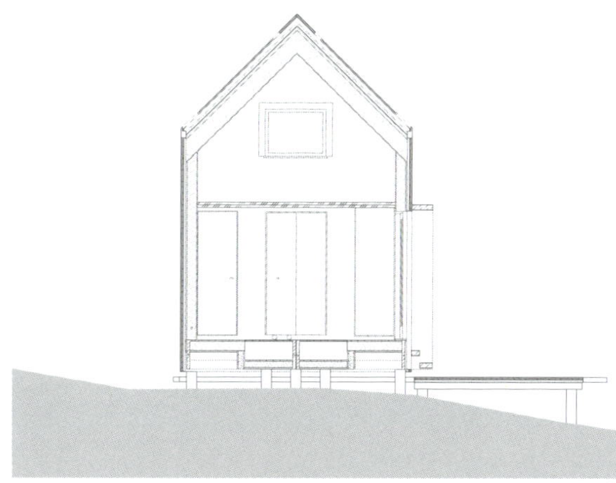

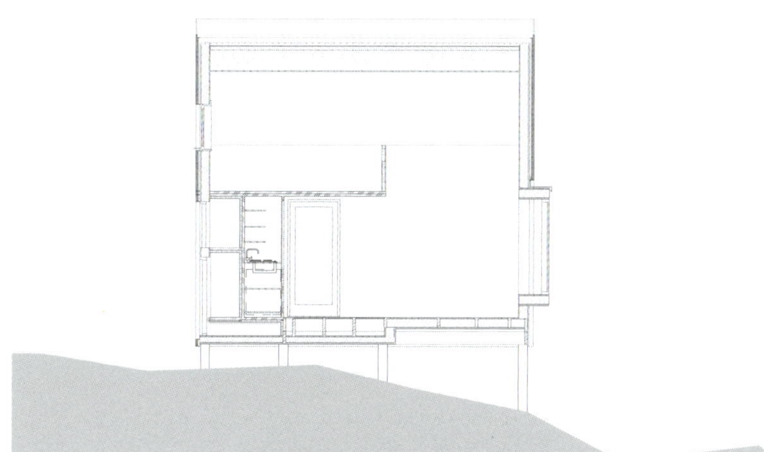

AURORA

Troms, Norway

Design
Snorre Stinessen Architecture

Completion
2024

Sustainable features
Natural materials; no plastic; minimal footprint

GFA
92 m^2

Photographer
Snorre Stinessen

Aurora is set in a beautiful location in the Lyngen alps. The main building is organized around a central entrance with a covered outdoor fireplace. It branches off to the kitchen, dining room and lounge on the north side, library and master bedroom around an open fireplace on the south side. A hidden entrance through the library leads to a comfortable bathroom and wardrobe on the south side. Three bedrooms are done as separate volumes with ensuite bathrooms. The main focus of the interior is the experience of the views, which is accentuated through the upwards steps in the floor, culminating in the bench by the slanting glass, high above ground. The building enables both privacy as well as exposure to the diverse nature, regardless of weather and season.

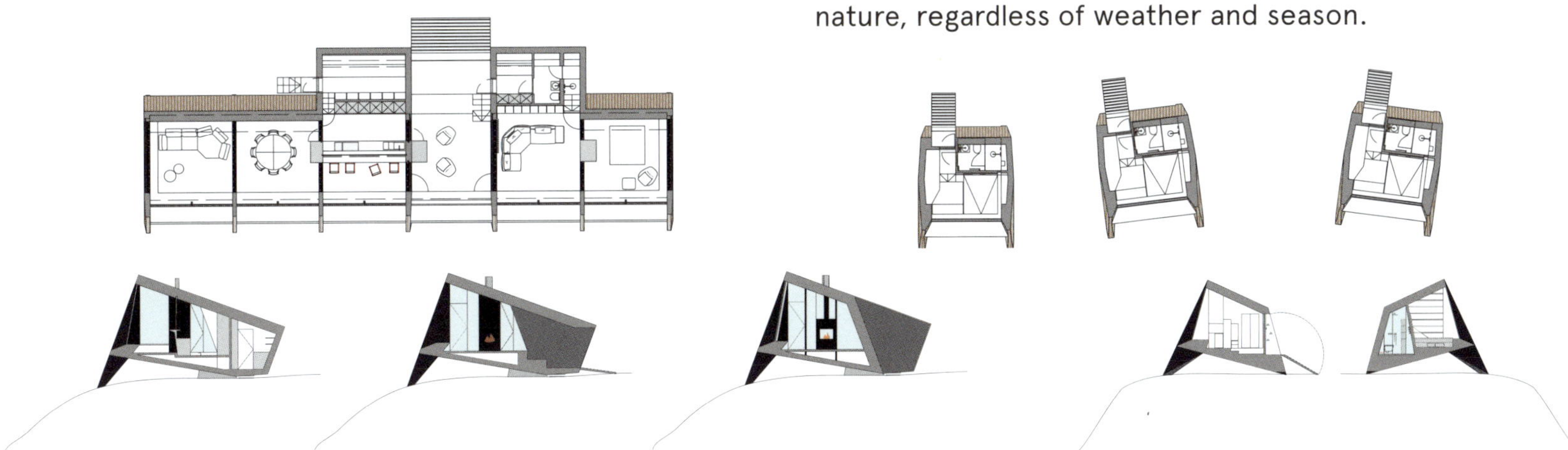

VILLA S – A WOODEN MONOLITH

Orust, Sweden

Design
Andersson & Stare Arkitekter

Completion
2023

Sustainable features
Wooden construction

GFA
195 m^2

Photographer
James Silverman (124–126,127 r., 128, 129),
Andersson & Stare (127 a., l.)

Villa S is perched on top of a mountain on the island of Orust, offering panoramic views of the fjord below. The wild Nordic landscape, with its raw granite outcrops, heather, and pine trees, creates a distinctive and untouched atmosphere. Considering the villa's natural surroundings, the architects took the form of two offset volumes, one placed higher and closer to the mountain surface and balancing the other. The house is also clad entirely in a uniform wooden paneling to harmonize with the nearby rock and pine trees. The pure, minimalist form gives it a modern and abstract character, like a monolith emerging from the mountain. The interior layout is distributed across the two volumes, with one housing private spaces and the other serving the social functions.

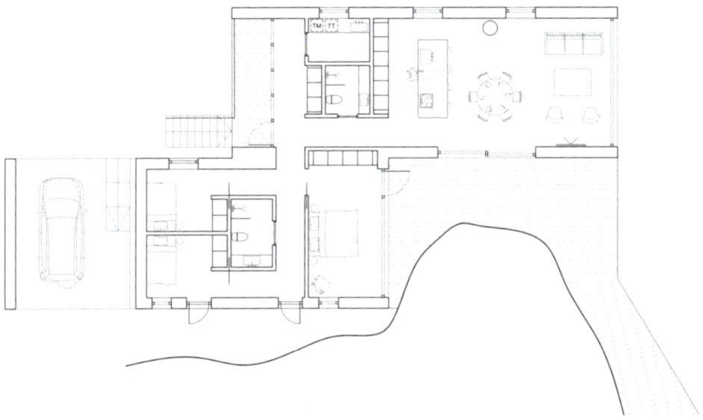

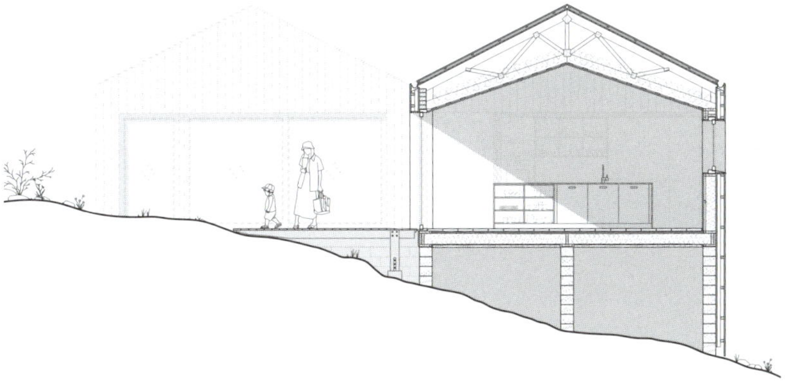

HOLIDAY HOME

Þingvallavatn, Iceland

Design
Krads

Completion
2020

Sustainable features
Green roof; locally sourced materials where possible; natural ventilation

GFA
145 m²

Photographer
Marino Thorlacius

The Holiday Home is carefully placed on a densely overgrown hill that is sloping north in the direction of the great Lake Þingvallavatn in southwestern Iceland. On multiple levels, the otherworldly landscape has modeled the form of the building. In dialogue with the terrain, the concrete foundation of the wooden house lies in three staggered planes that follow the movement of the landscape. In a similar manner, the roof surface, overgrown with local grass and moss, slopes partly towards and partly with the hill. The location of the house has been chosen with great care to integrate the building into the surroundings while framing specially selected views of the landscape.

VILLA AUSTEVOLL

Selbjørn, Norway

Design
Saunders Architecture

Completion
2020

GFA
285 m^2

Photographer
Ivar Kvaal

Villa Austevoll is situated on the island of Selbjørn, south of Bergen. The goal was to create a cabin that forms a shelter as well as an observatory for views, yet has an unusual, modern look. The house was lifted above the landscape to protect it and take advantage of the hill-side site's views. The main body has a cross-like form and sits on top of a recessed plinth. A triangular concrete slice recesses into the hillside. Slim steel pillars complement its supportive function. The plinth holds the entrance hall, utility spaces, and a spiral staircase. One wing houses the living room, including a library wall, while the other hosts the kitchen. Overall, the aim was to balance a simplicity within the layout and low-maintenance interior materials, considering the coastal conditions and hillside position.

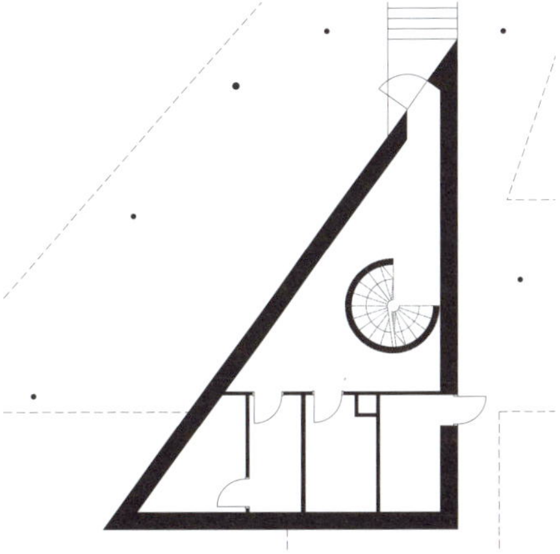

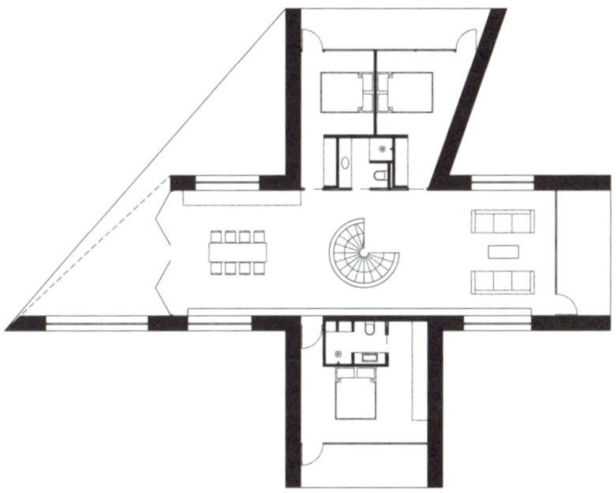

HEATHER-HILL BEACH HOUSE

Vejby, Denmark

Design
Norm Architects

Completion
2024

Sustainable features
Sedum green roof; cedar cladding

GFA
232 m^2

Photographer
Jonas Bjerre-Poulsen

Heatherhill Beach House is gently nestled among rolling dunes along the Kattegat coast in northern Denmark. The house follows the natural slope of the landscape, with timber-clad volumes rising subtly from the ground and framing selected views of the surrounding hills and sea. Cedar cladding develops a silvery patina over time, blending the home with its environment, while a sedum roof reinforces its connection to nature. Inside, materials like Douglas Fir and natural brick create warmth and continuity with the outdoors. The design balances openness and privacy, allowing light and views to shape the experience, making Heatherhill Beach House a tranquil retreat intimately connected to its landscape.

PANORAMA HYTTENE

Sandve, Norway

Design
Holon arkitektur

Interior Design
Byggmester Helge Kvale and Tove Virata Bråthen

Completion
2024

GFA
22 m^2 each

Photographer
Ida Kristin Vollum (142–144), Jone Torkelsen (145)

HAKON

Panorama Hyttene on the west coast of Norway has a unique location on the edge of the North Sea. The mission was to design three luxury micro cabins with a modern architectural style that would provide the most exceptional accommodation experiences. This was achieved through utilizing the natural surroundings and spectacular views that the area has to offer. For instance, the location offers an excellent view of the northern lights. The architects designed the cabins as elements within the landscape, inspired by the moving stones from Ice Age, and the surrounding rock formations in which the cabins are situated. The large windows that lean over the landscape towards the horizon, along with the dark interior, invite the guests to enjoy the beautiful view.

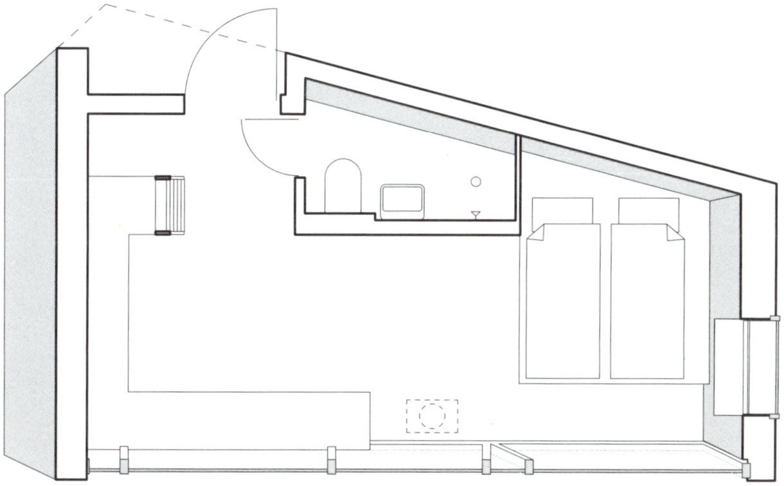

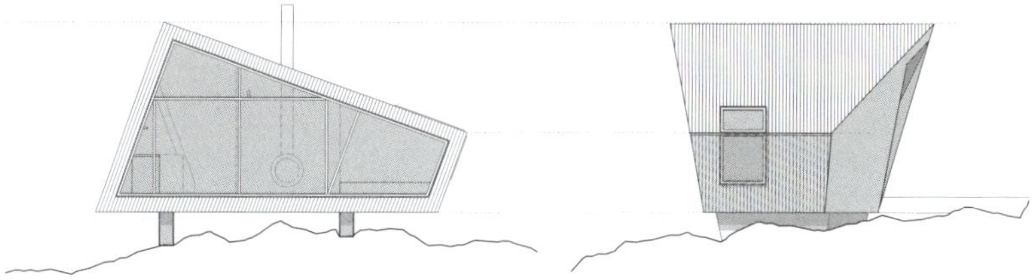

VILLA E

Aarhus, Denmark

Design
C.F. Møller Architects

Completion
2020

GFA
261 m^2

Sustainable features
Simple, durable and well-chosen materials such as brick, oak, and natural stone; sustainable wooden structure; built according to Dansk Energiklasse 2020

Photographer
Julian Weyer

THE GRAND TOUR

Villa E is located in an undulating district of small houses in northern Aarhus. The villa´s composition consists of four simple saddle roof houses, which together form the framework. The main architectural approach unfolds in a larger main house, which has been raised up onto three smaller buildings on two levels. A distinctive brick staircase leads up to the entrance. This opens into the villa's main room, a large kitchen family room with a high and elegantly curved ceiling, finished with a skylight that creates fantastic light. The kitchen is built into a brick core that runs throughout the house and together with a window seat, forms sculptural elements. The living room has a sloping ceiling, lined with moldings, which creates a covered living space.

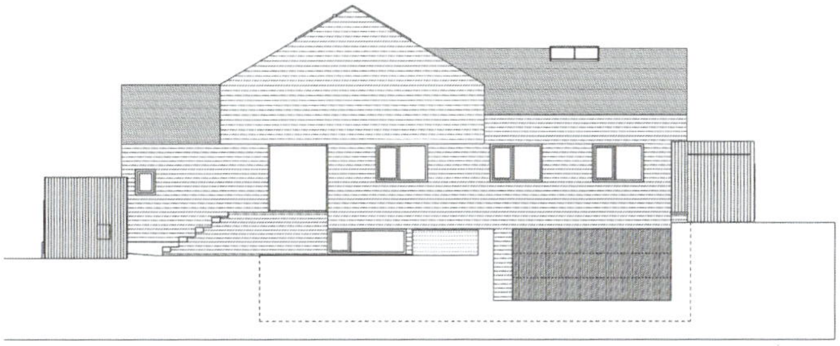

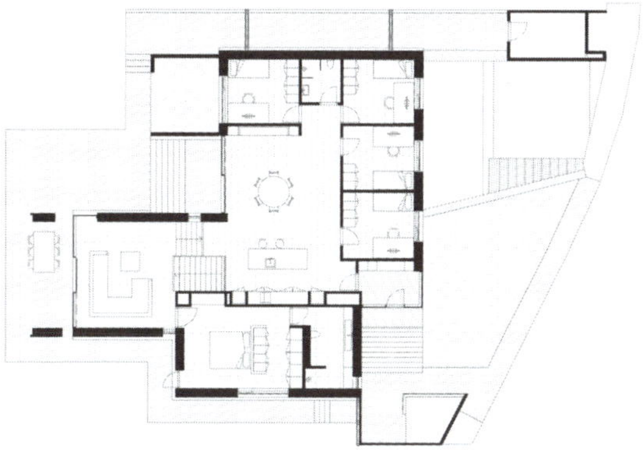

HOUSE ON PILLARS

Nesodden, Norway

Design
Sanden+Hodnekvam Architects

Completion
2022

GFA
114 m^2

Photographer
Thomas Ekstrøm (152, 154), Sanden+Hodnekvam (153, 155)

House on Pillars is located on the peninsula Nesodden, south of Oslo. The long, narrow house is carefully lodged between existing rocks and trees. It is raised on wooden pillars to respect the landscape. The site´s natural topography creates multiple outdoor spaces with outlooks into the rock bed and treetops. The distinct load bearing structure is visible in the exterior and interior. It elevates the building from the landscape. The building´s open plan and connection to the environment give the impression of a large surrounding, while sliding doors create private spheres. An open space with daylight is in the center of the house with a glass roof and windows towards the fjord and garden. Walls and floors are covered in pine, with recycled brick floors in the winter garden and living room.

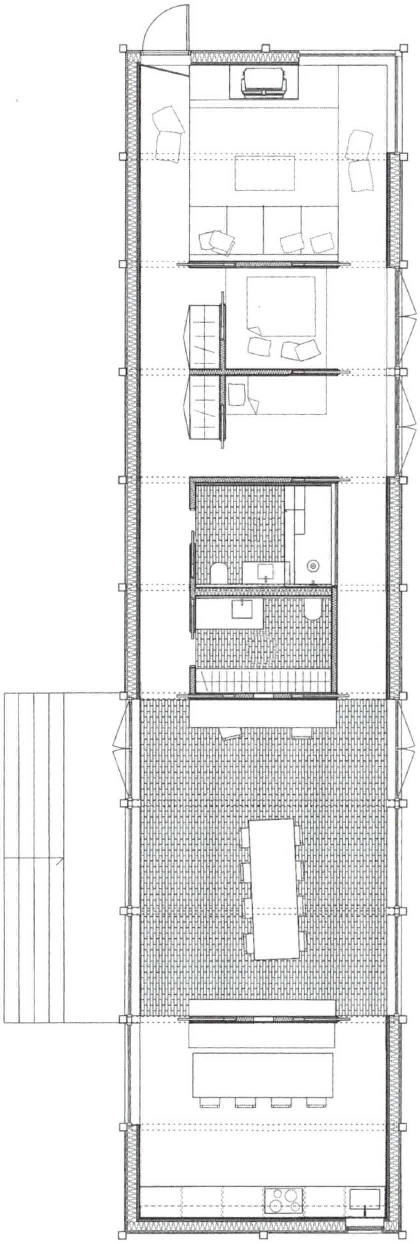

VILLA KOPPAR

Helsinki, Finland

Design
Collaboratorio

Completion
2023

Sustainable features
Straw wall elements; earth floor; clay plaster; wooden façade

GFA
180 m^2

Photographer
Simone Bossi (156, 157, 158 r.b., 159), Niclas Mäkelä (158 l., r.a.)

Villa Koppar sits within the rugged natural setting of Kopparnäs, Inkoo, about 45 kilometers west of Helsinki. The project comprises two buildings: the main house and a garage with a small dependance. The fully ecological, geothermally heated passive house was designed for a young and growing family with a modest budget. Built with a prefabricated straw building system, its exterior is clad in Organowood spruce, and the interiors are lined with clay plaster. Living spaces and a landscape sauna occupy the upper floor, where large openings and a generous terrace embrace views of the surrounding terrain. The interiors and lighting follow a restrained, minimalist approach, shaped by wood and clay as primary materials. Both floors are constructed in rammed earth.

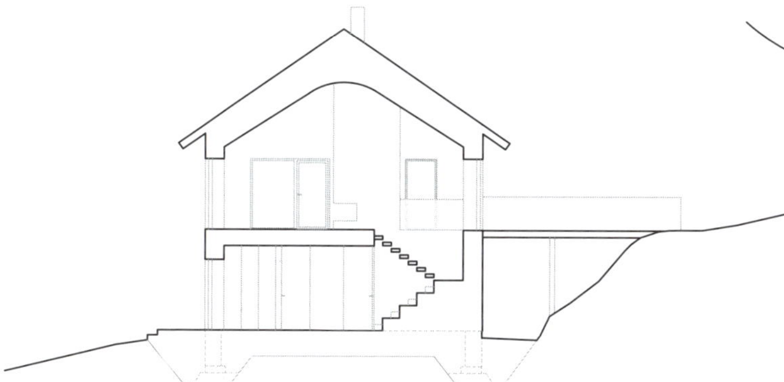

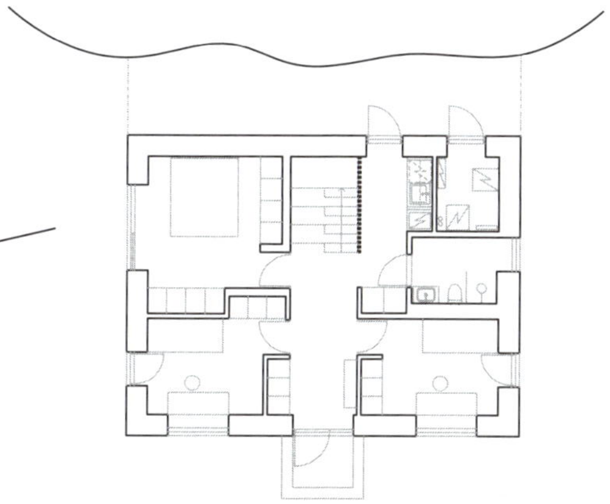

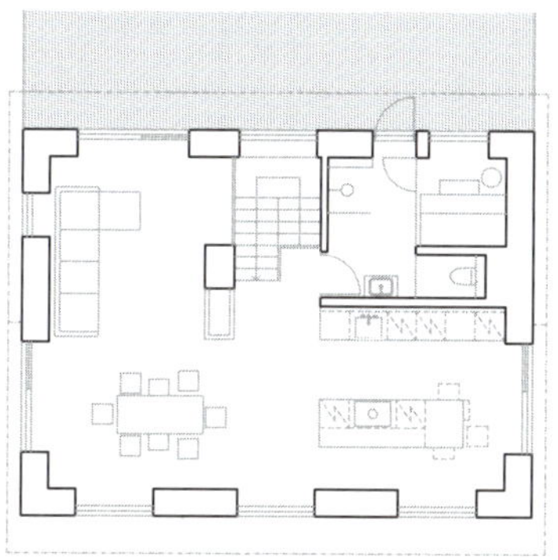

HYTTE HELLESTØ

Byberg, Norway

Design
Helen & Hard

Completion
2023

GFA
80 m^2

Photographer
Sindre Ellingsen

Hytte Hellestø is located at one of Norway's most beautiful sandy beaches on the edge of grass-covered sand dunes. The goal was to carefully integrate the vacation home into the landscape so that it feels like a natural part and extension of the dunes. A three-part, continuous panoramic window offers a 180-degree-view directly towards the open sea and the expansive beaches. The vacation home gives a sense of spaciousness. Glass walls and windows divide the space into different zones, creating a continuous feeling of openness despite its modest size. A parametrically shaped, wave-like ceiling mirrors the motif of ocean waves and softly fades out. The entire interior and all furniture are custom-made from oak wood specifically for this space.

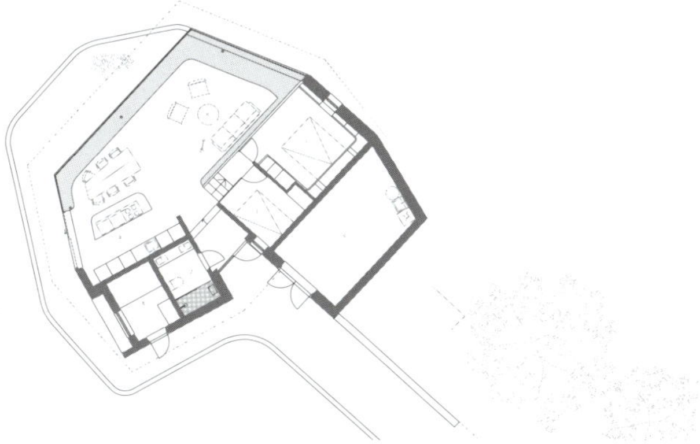

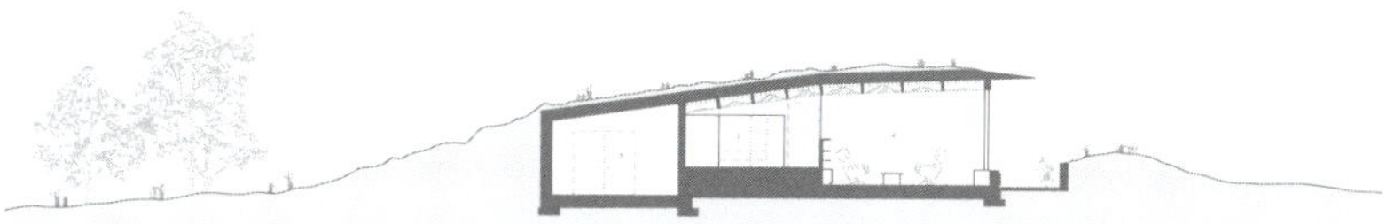

VILLA BUTTER

Western Gotland, Sweden

Design
Ateljé Ö

Garden design
Anna Winsnes

Completion
2022

Sustainable features
Locally sourced high-quality materials

GFA
250 m^2

Photographer
Erik Lefvander

What first catches the visitor's eye when arriving at the heavy structure of Villa Butter is the spectacular view. The project sits right on the edge of a 20-meter-cliff overlooking the ocean. But more vital to how the project was designed and planned is the beautiful grove the house sits in. The materials used are oak, concrete, glass, and copper. A lot of work was put into finding the perfect cement, render, and application technique to achieve the right texture for the façade. The project is designed with an obvious rhythm, while the floor plan is based on the program. This means that the sub-areas are not subordinate to an overall form, but rather expand and take shape differently according to their various functions. Villa Butter is a grand project but with a humble persona.

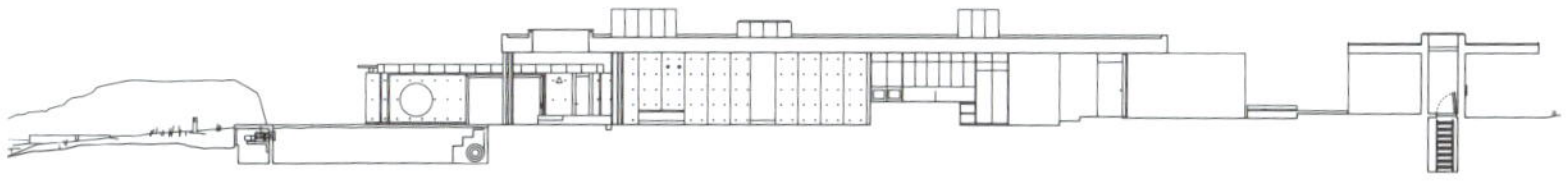

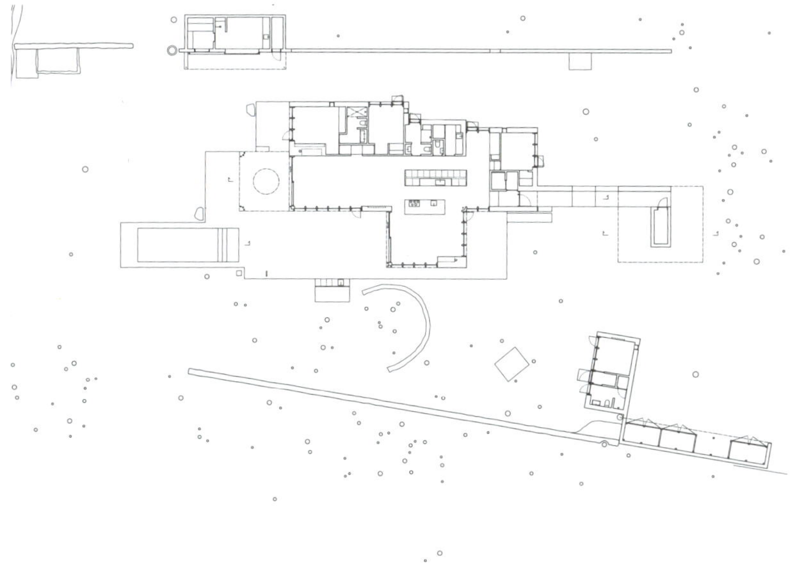

L15 HOUSE

Lillesand, Norway

Design
SRA / Sunniva Rosenberg Arkitektur

Completion
2020

GFA
72 m^2

Photographer
Rasmus Norlander (168), Sunniva Rosenberg (169–171)

L15 House is located in Lillesand, a small town close to the Norwegian south coast. The extension provides an open plan dining kitchen and living area, as well as an outdoor dining area that looks out over the garden. The architect placed value on including the building into its natural surroundings sustainably by combining good craftmanship and durable materials. Selecting neutral colors for the building, the idyllic garden with its indigenous pine trees and rocky landscape remains the main focus. The angular plan opens up in three directions. It creates new outdoor spaces and connects the house to the cultivated garden, which allows rays of sunshine in. In contrast to the existing house, the extension has a star-shaped plan designed to open up views to the garden.

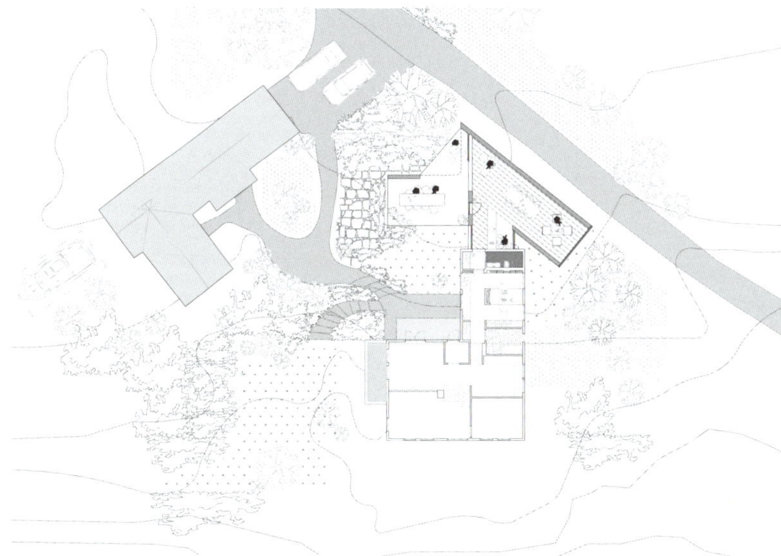

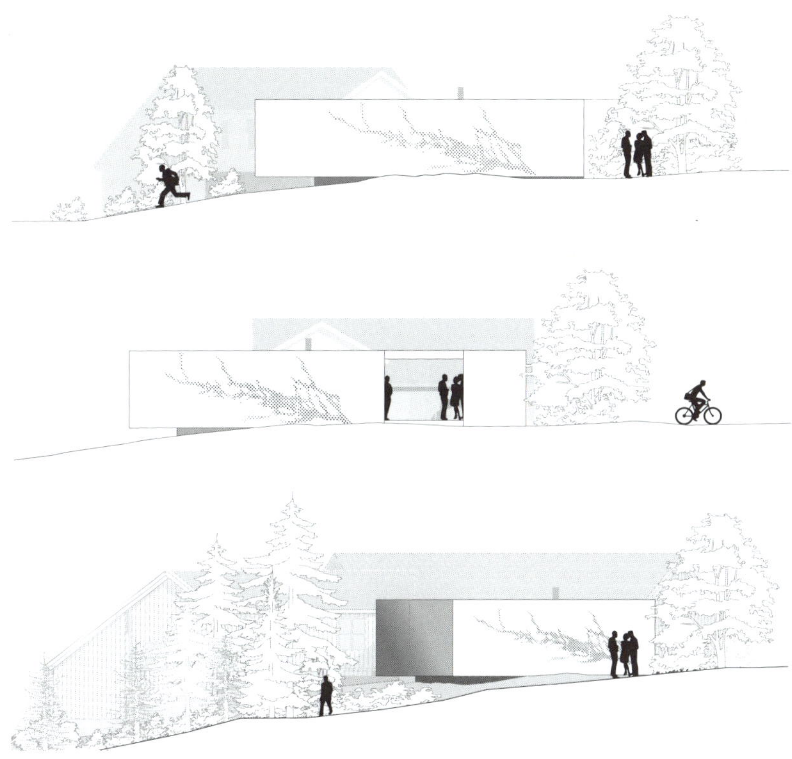

KLÖVER-VÄGEN

Stockholm, Sweden

Design
Kaminsky Architektur

Completion
2024

Original building
1974

GFA
75 m^2

Photographer
Emil Fagander

A classic Swedish brick house from 1974 has been transformed with the addition of an orangery. This elegant glass structure extends the outdoor season, offering space for cultivation and family life. A former balcony was replaced by a deeper two-level volume with generous openings to merge indoors with the out. A new entrance and larger hallway help to improve function. The larch wood cladding softens the brick exterior and will age in harmony with the warm-toned, treated timber frames. The addition has also given the house a new entrance situation and a larger hall with space for more storage. Furthermore, the new wooden façade gives the house a softer, warmer expression and creates a welcoming entrance side facing south.

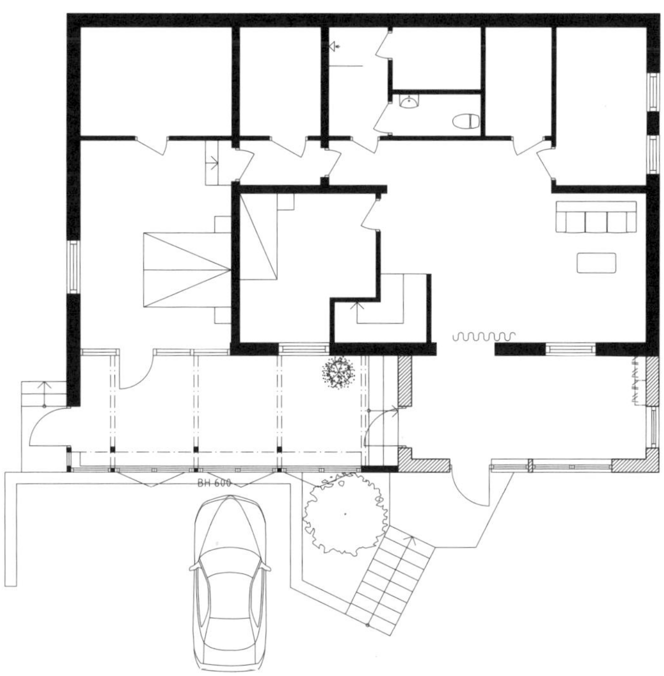

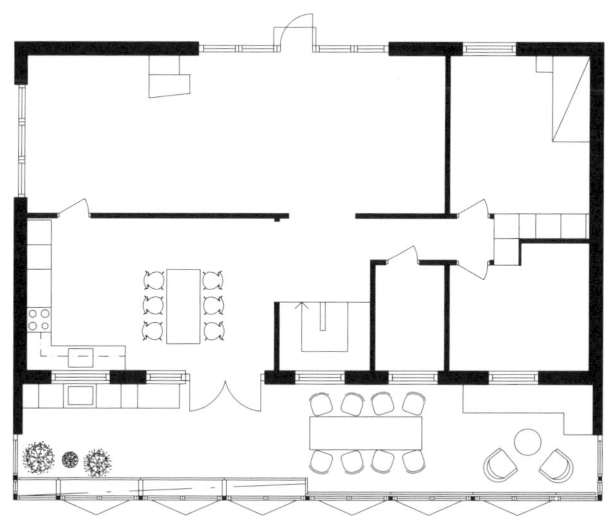

ÅSTRUP HAVE

Haderslev, Denmark

Design
NORRØN Architects

Completion
2020

Sustainable features
Roof profile allows for solar panels; ventilation; chimneys; skylights; modern technology

GFA
600 m^2

Photographer
Torben Eskerod

Åstrup Have is a new recreational farmhouse gazing at Haderslev Fjord. Organized around a central patio that unifies the wings of the building, Åstrup Have stands as a four-legged concrete structure. The clustered volumes are constructed from raw concrete panels with brass-filled joints. Resembling a golden relief carved into the raw concrete panels, the brass-fillings soften the building. As a homage to local, Schleswig tradition, the steep roof unfolds as a thatched structure and a binding tissue. The interior spaces are composed as a series of diverse spaces, varying in height and size, and throughout the building, a sacred and harmonized atmosphere has been sought. The main programs of the building consist of production, educational spaces, and a kitchen.

BOAT HOUSE

Isle of Sokn, Norway

Design
Espen Surnevik

Completion
2020

Sustainable features
Reuse of historic stone foundations; local materials; flood-resilient; climate-adapted design

GFA
96 m^2

Photographer
Rasmus Norlander

The Boat House sits on the Norwegian coast atop 200-year-old stone foundations that reflect the local landscape. The new wooden superstructure follows the original roof angles, clad in oxidized zinc, while spruce and pine interiors continue local material traditions and custom furniture adapts to occasional flooding. Old and new meet in a dialogue of stone, timber, and modern technologies, exploring heritage, sustainability, and contemporary living. The Boat House preserves the story of the place while offering a modern holiday home in its maritime surroundings.

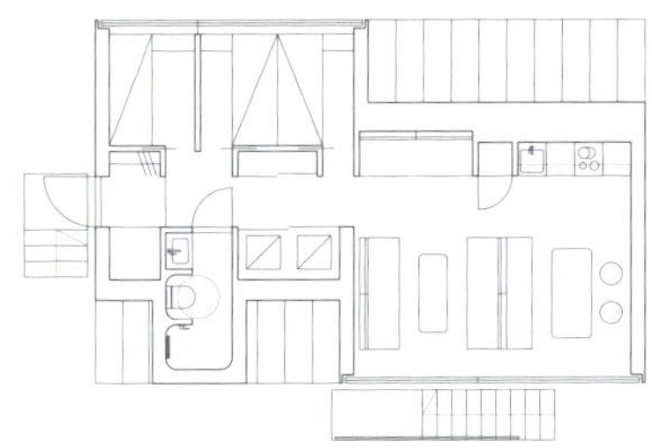

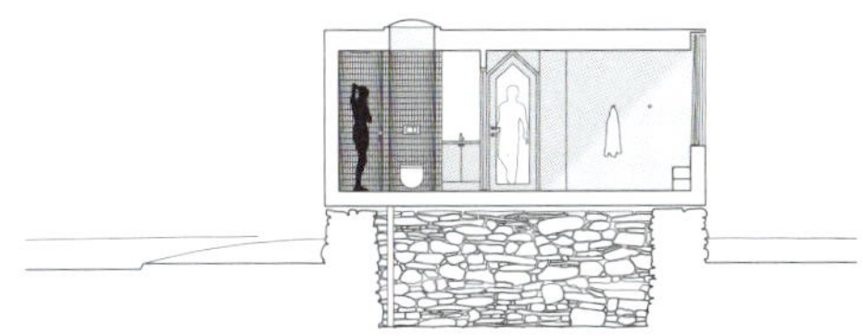

A FRAME SKI-LODGE

Åre, Sweden

Design
Måns Tham Arkitektkontor

Completion
2022

GFA
220 m^2

Photographer
Staffan Andersson

The A-Frame Ski Lodge is built with prefabricated A-frames and curved dormer windows. Its triangular shape resembles a small mountain, blurring the line between house and ground as snow piles up. The tent-like form is traditional, but dormers bring light into the 25-meter-long house and create usable space upstairs. The building is divided into five sections, with gable ends left dormer-free to preserve the shape, while asymmetrical curved dormers align with the overall form and echo the surrounding trees. The entrance on the northern façade works as a camera aperture with glazed views straight through the building to the sunken terrace with valley views. The landing has curved ski storages, emphasizing the flow through the house. Upstairs there are two identical suites with five beds each and a tent-like gable room, one facing morning sun and the other afternoon light.

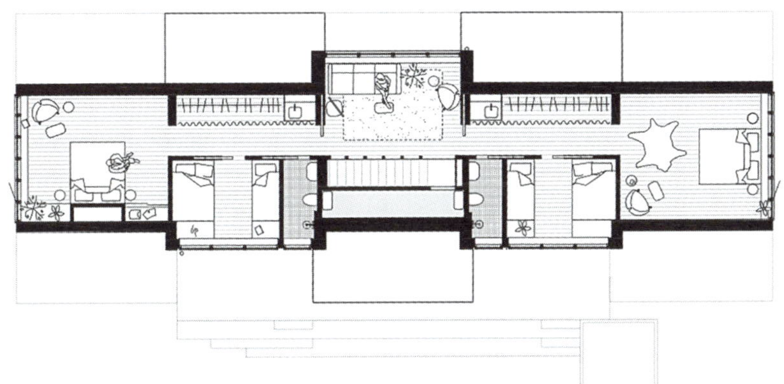

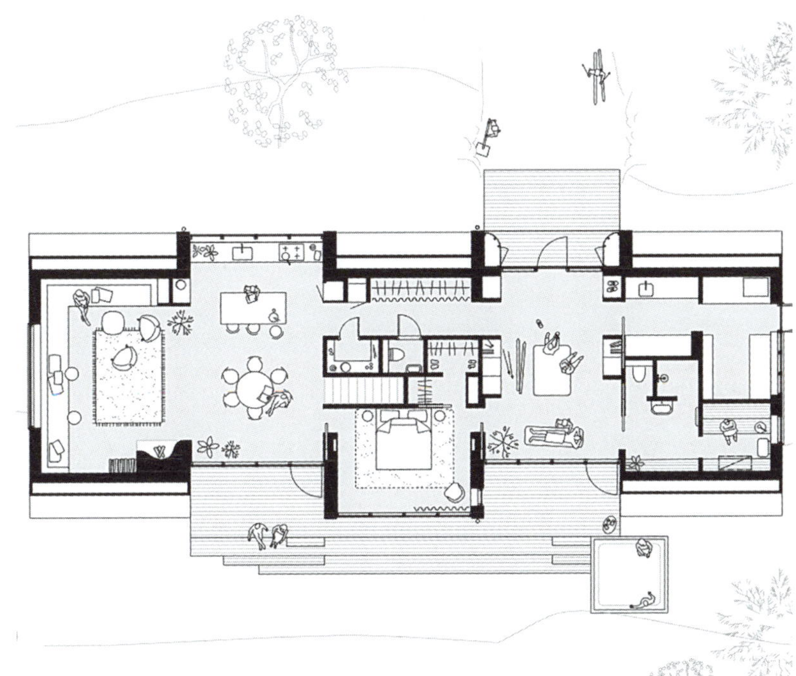

Index

The Deutsche Nationalbibliothek lists this publication in the Deutsche Nationalbibliografie; detailed bibliographic data are available in the Internet at http://dnb.dnb.de

ISBN 978-3-03768-309-5

www.braun-publishing.ch

1st edition 2026

Project coordination: Editorial office van Uffelen
Editorial staff and layout: Emily Altintas, Katja Raab
Graphic concept: Sarah-Lea Hipp
Reproduction: Bild1Druck, Berlin

Product Safety
Publisher: Braun Publishing AG, Arenenbergstr. 2, 8268 Salenstein, Switzerland
publisher@braun-publishing.ch
EU-Representative: Bookwise GmbH, Zeppelinstr. 67, 81669 Munich, Germany
info@bookwise.de